Cc

1
Preface

PART ONE
Mainly by coach or car

3
Chapter One
France: A family under canvas

6
Chapter Two
Macedonia or North Macedonia

33
Chapter Three
Malaysia: Deep jungle and skyscraper hotels

PART TWO
Mainly by train

43
Chapter Four
India: Touring Rajahstan on the
Toy Train and the Palace on wheels

76
Chapter Five
South Africa: Political prisoners,
frightened monkeys and dinner in a cave

PART THREE
Mainly by ocean or river cruising

85
Chapter Six
Bali: A short cruise, where we meet
a dangerous lizard

92
Chapter Seven
An Adriatic Odyssey: A cruise aboard Minerva 2014

127
Chapter Eight
Russia by river from Moscow to St Petersburg

136
Chapter Nine
The Bahamas: A rush for better seats

139
Chapter Ten
The Maldives: An endangered tropical paradise

TRAVELLERS' TALES

Published by Alderley Publishing
England

ISBN 978-1-84396-642-5

Also available as a Kindle ebook
ISBN 978-1-84396-643-2

Typesetting and pre-press production
eBook Versions
27 Old Gloucester Street
London WC1N 3AX
www.ebookversions.com

TRAVELLERS' TALES

Derek & Barbara Torrington

Alderley Publishing

142
Chapter Eleven
Flowers of the Aegean: A cruise aboard Minerva

181
Chapter Twelve
An odd one: Iceland all in one day

Preface

We have been able to visit 65 different countries since we married in 1965, all of them leaving us with pleasant memories, from our early holidays of camping in France with our children in the 1950s to the two of us travelling on the "Toy train" to the foothills of the Himalayas where the government of British India moved during the intense heat of the summer, before changing to "The Palace on Wheels" for a tour of Rajahstan, with its many examples of the luxurious lifestyle of the Rajahs and their wonderful palaces – with hints of the now outlawed practice of suttee, requiring a wife to immolate herself by jumping on to her husband's funeral pyre.

At another extreme we travelled by river from Moscow to Saint Petersburg at a time when Russia was emerging from Communist rule to re-establish herself in a different type of society.

Although not included here, we travelled in many European countries, including Norway, Austria, Italy, Germany, Spain and Portugal.

In the hope of providing a good read we have put together 12 samples of what we hope will be an interesting, and occasionally entertaining of where we have been, and what we found when we got there.

Derek & Barbara Torrington
June 2021

Part One

Mainly by coach or car

Chapter 1
France A family under canvas

Although we had both visited when we were single, now we are married and have four children, aged from 6 to 11. We return to France, this time to camp. n on holiday with her parents in a caravan, but neither of us had ever lived under canvas.

A friend of ours who did camp under canvas mentioned that in his own travels he had been next to David Sheppard using the facilities of a company called "Canvas Holidays", who made all the arrangements of booking a site, erecting a tent, equipping it with beds, tables, chairs, cooking arrangements etc. and finally booked a channel crossing for the car.

I thought that if it was good enough for an England test cricketer, it was good enough for us and we made our arrangements and set off, across the Channel and to a Paris suburb to spend three nights under canvas as at base for travelling daily into Paris on the Metro for sight seeing and lunching a different restaurants or discovering the joy of eating baguettes or pommes frites each day.

The highlight was Montmartre with its narrow winding streets artists on the Place du tertre and the Sacre Coeur crowning it all. Much more recently built than most other churches in Paris, it has an intriguing history. The French went to war with Prussia inn 1870 (the Franco Prussian war) and two Catholic businessmen made a vow that if Paris was spared in the conflict, they would build a great church dedicated to the Sacred Heart of Christ. Although Paris suffered a lengthy siege it was spared destruction and the church was built with the support of the Archbishop of Paris. Work began in 1875 and was completed in 1914 but not consecrated until 1919 due the First World War.

From Paris there we drove down to the coast at La Boule and another Canvas holidays tent. At both sites we had the same sleeping arrangements: a reasonably solid double camp bed for the parents on one side with a screen, and on the other side, similarly screened, was a space for four less solid camp beds which the children called "super bendy".

Anyone travelling from Cheshire to camp in France during high summer does so pretty sure that the weather will be fine and sunny. They would have been dead wrong this year. A Canvas Holidays tent was set on a groundsheet, that was waterproof, on the bare ground. When it rained, as it did quite often, you were dry inside the tent, but the ground underneath you became soft mud. This could be further complicated by burrowing voles. Altogether this produced a soft uneven surface beneath your feet.

There was a separate, solid amenity block for all users of the site for ablutions and laundry. We continued for several years with Canvas Holidays in France and Italy. facilities improved with competition from companies like Eurocamp and Keycamp. Both our daughters had summer holiday jobs as couriers on the sites and our younger son met his future wife while working for Keycamp, although it was thirty years before they married!

However our main problem on that first trip was a fishermen's strike in France, during which they blockaded the ports. having arrived in France at Calais, we now had to drive to Rotterdam and take a crossing to Felixstowe. We set off very early, and drove and drove until we eventually arrived after 500 miles, not at Rotterdam, but at the queue of dozens of others doing the same thing, and our crossing to Felixstowe finally began at 1.00 am the following day.

Chapter 2
Macedonia or north Macedonia

Before we start, you may well be asking where Macedonia is. Geographically it is a Baltic state, below Kosovo and opposite Albania. It used to be part of the old Yugoslavia. The name Macedonia had long been disputed by Greece as they regard the name is valid only for territory in Greece. By 2019 there was agreement that the country would henceforth be called "North Macedonia".

The attraction of visiting (North) Macedonia was to see some of the murals in the many Byzantine churches. We travelled as part of a group run by travel agent Cox and Kings. Now for our story....

At 4.15 as the alarm went off. Somewhat bleary eyed, we dressed, had toast and set off to the "meet and greet" at terminal 2 of Manchester Airport, We left the car and its keys in their care and went on to check in ourselves and the bag through to Skopje and went to find the lounge. There wasn't a great deal on offer but the juice and coffee kept us going till we were on the plane. The flight to Prague was uneventful; the breakfast ok, as was the service.

Changing planes in Munich was remarkably easy; we

walked off one plane, round the corner, to the other plane that was already boarding. We were in the very comfortable front seats and with a charming steward who plied us with sparkling wine and found a vegetarian lunch for Barbara. Again the flight was uneventful and we were soon in Skopje, collecting our case and going out to see the Cox and Kings representative directing us to a waiting spot where we met our delightful young guides, Mia and Alex (known as Ace)

As we drove away we were able to see the 66metres high Millennium cross on the top of the highest hill in the area. Also flying alongside the cross were two flags, a green Islamic one and an Albanian one. Both of these are controversial in Macedonia because they are now very separate from and Albania, and Islam is the minority religion, but Skopje is very close to the border which is still disputed. The southern border is also tricky as it is with Greece who still didn't recognise Macedonia and would not allow any aircraft to fly over their country and is mounting a determined opposition to it joining the EU.(.Accession talks to the EU eventually began in 20/20 but are currently blocked by Bulgaria.)

Our route took us past Tetovo and on to Gostivar. We were kept informed about the conflict with Albania around Tetovo in 2000 which caused many Macedonians to leave the town and the university. Just south of Gostivar we had a "pit" stop; Coffee was provided by Mia; this was one of the many thoughtful actions she or Ace provided on the trip. They had also been to the stop earlier to make sure the toilets were clean! Another thing was to arrange for Barbara to have a vegetarian meal. The locals were big meat eaters and chefs had never come across vegetarians, so Ace phoned ahead each evening to the restaurants we were visiting the next day to warn the chef, then he carried a small green cloth that he put on the table by Barbara to identify her.

We were soon on our way again and a sign of things in Macedonia were glimpses of the agriculture of the area. In the season tobacco was an important crop. Apples and tomatoes are also widely grown. the flat land gave way to the mountains and the rain increased. We passed huge quarries; poor farms with one or two tethered cows. As we approached Ohrid there were more vineyards.. We could see little of the lake because of the mist and rain but the Millennium Palace Hotel appeared and seemed quite nice, not exciting, but ok. Our room, 208 was on the second floor. It was a twin room with a walk in shower etc.. We sorted ourselves out and met up with everyone else in the foyer to be taken by minibus to the restaurant for dinner. wet! Dinner was good, pleasant company, good food especially for a vegetarian with her little green card placed carefully beside the place mat.

Next day we arrived for breakfast by 8am, finding the dining room deserted. where was everyone? Were we the first? It seemed like it; so we collected cutlery, juice etc. and then milk, which proved to be yogurt..The hot food was tepid at best and we made rather tentative choices onto cold plates. By this time others were arriving and looking rather bemused. We were not impressed with our first Macedonian breakfast.

Before getting on the minibus for our excursion we wandered along the lake which was pleasant, with small colourful fishing boats half hidden in the reeds, and gulls and coots swimming on the water, we would have liked the opportunity to go further and into the little town.

The first stop on our excursion was the old gate to the city of Ohrid and through it to the 13th century church of Sveta Bogorodica Perivleptos, our first sight of the delightful architecture of the Macedonian churches. We were to see many more, and we never ceased to delight in them. This first was dedicated to St. Clement when his remains were transferred to the church during the Ottoman Empire. We were met at the entrance by the most extraordinary custodian of the place. She was dressed in what looked like a black jump suit with a white belt and elaborate silver decoration, a black cap sitting on black hair in braided plaits. She had a huge personality, was immensely proud of her church and of her published research of it. She was an acclaimed authority on the church and had no fewer than eight academic publications – counted on fingers for extra emphasis!

The interior was truly amazing; it was covered in vibrant coloured frescoes. The belief in the old Orthodox Church is that it (and the person) should be plain on the outside but glorious inside to show the glory of Christ and that our beauty also comes from within; they followed this pattern faithfully. Every surface inside was covered with painting in ways that we came to understand and appreciate. They apparently represent a unique achievement in medieval painting. One of them, showing the scene in the Garden of Gethsemane, depicts the mourners in depth and perspective, something that would be lost for centuries.

In the dome there is always Christ looking down on the

worshippers and holding the bible; in the apse always the Virgin, a very important person in the Orthodox Church. Below the Virgin is a scene of the Communion of the Apostles, in two halves so that you see the serving of both the bread and wine. Between the windows are the Old Testament prophets and on a lower row the monks of local importance and on the columns, the Saints, some of whom we came to recognise over the week.

We could have spent a long time in that church but we had to move on to the icon museum. The icons were lovely, well displayed and lit. We particularly liked St. Marina who had the devil by the hair threatening to chop off his head; he looked terrified while protecting his genitals. From there we walked to Tsar Samoil's Fortress, which dates from the 10th century but records suggest that a fort has occupied the top of Ohrid hill since at least the 3rd century. Until the Ottomans arrived in 1395 the town and its inhabitants existed within the walls. Just inside was a 2000 year old ampitheatre, buried for years till the 20th century and was fully uncovered in 1990. It is used in the summer for concerts, as it was 2000 years ago.

We then walked along an uneven track from which we had super, though misty, views over the lake We were heading for *St*. Kliment at Plaosnik, a modern reconstruction in the old Byzantine style, a splendid church that has been renovated and enlarged three times in the 12th, 13th and 14th centuries. We stood a little way from the church so we could see the whole site; this allowed us to appreciate the remains of the 10th century first European university. It was founded by St. Clement and St. Naum. Soon after it was founded 3000 students were believed to be studying there, a real centre of education. On the same site is a rather nice mosaic, only recently discovered.

We climbed up the path to the top of the hill and then down steep, uneven steps and down a very difficult path through the woods, emerging to the most beautiful sight, a tiny chapel perched on the edge of a cliff with a back drop of the lake. It was the church of St. John built in 1270. Inside it was dark and guarded by its caretaker who was very strict about the ban on photos which was pity because there weren't any postcards of the unusual frescoes. The same carer of the church also dispensed a fierce locally brewed spirit from a plastic bottle!

There was another walk down a steep path to the edge of the lake. Here we boarded, very precariously, a small boat and we set sail across the lake to Ohrid town. The views of St. John's and of the fishing boats and the town were certainly worth the difficulty of getting in the boat.

In town we had most welcome cup of coffee and a short sit down but not for long because it was then off to St. Sofia, just by the café. The guide book claims this is the biggest and most significant In Ohrid. Built in the 9th/10th century and for a long time the cathedral church, today it hosts many cultural events in the summer.

The frescoes are the largest surviving in the world; they had survived the Turks who had destroyed the dome and the capitol of the church. The Virgin is seen in the apse and Christ in the dome in the garments of the Archbishop which is seen as blessing the new church; below, Christ and angels brought down the liturgy of the Eastern Orthodox Church. To the left of the altar is the Communion of the Apostles who have their hands covered as a sign of holiness; to the right the Trinity.

Another fragment of 11th-century fresco shows the Virgin Mary with her legs crossed *and* with bare knees – apparently most unusual. Also a gruesome scene showed a pile of bodies, the death of 40 people who were tortured to death.

We walked down through the old town past the tiny hospital church, where those in quarantine were kept. It occupied a quiet green oasis in the narrow cobbled streets At the harbour there was a rather nice boat waiting for us to board.fora sunny picturesque two hour experience. By now it was 2.30, pm, we hadn't had any lunch and we were all feeling hungry. Mia had anticipated this while in Ohrid and had bought a large box of bananas and a supply of varied and delicious breads. We all enjoyed them, there wasn't much left within half an hour. Being British we determinedly sat outside, chatting and watching the passing scenery in the decidedly chilly, misty/wet afternoon. The captain couldn't understand us and kept inviting us into the warmth down below. Gradually, one by one we gave in and went down; it was lovely.

We arrived at St. Naum's in the rain and walked up and into the monastery grounds through a two columned arch. We went immediately to lunch, which had been prepared for some time as we were late. We had taken the edge off our appetites with our snack aboard. Nevertheless we managed very good soup followed by beef (not so good) or vegetarian (very good) and pudding. The dining room was part of what was originally the monks' quarters, now a hotel and had a welcoming log fire burning.

As soon as we finished lunch we were whisked off to the church. It was built originally in the 10th century but through the centuries was destroyed several times and rebuilt in in its present form by the Turks. St. Naum was, in the 900s, a lecturer, teacher, healer and miracle-worker much loved by the local people as well as those from further away. The interior of the church is covered by 19th-century frescoes depicting the life of St. Naum.

One memorable scene depicted a bear that had been terrorising the villagers so they appealed to St. Naum to do something about it. He caught the bear and as punishment made him pull the village cart. This demeaning task was graphically represented in the icon. There was one beautiful, wooden icon of the Saint holding the bible and with the typical three fingers raised giving the blessing. The carving on the iconostasis was intricate and decorative. One strange feature inside was the grave of St. Naum where it is said if you go down on one knee and put your ear to the grave you can hear his heart beating still. We had an interesting run, seeing more of the countryside and the coast back to the hotel. It had been a really interesting day, very full and tiring but we had seen an impressive amount in just a few hours.

The next day we were going to Bitola, the second city of Macedonia. It was raining as we set off, rained all day and rained on the way back. We didn't see the famous national park set up by Tito and an umbrella had to be purchased to shelter from the rain! Apart from the rain it was an interesting journey with bits of history by our guide and intriguing countryside. We learned that the Turks had no university till 1900s; Macedonia had no rubbish collection till recently; there was much poverty especially among the gypsy community whose children didn't go to school but were sent out collecting glass bottles for the money they got on returning them; when this ceased and everything went plastic and their poverty was even worse.

On the flat plain the farms we passed grew apples and vines; hay was in dome shaped haystacks; honey was produced from the many hives we saw. Some of the power came from small hydro-electric power stations below the dams on the small streams. The guide produced a memorable quote about the area we were driving through "flat plains squashed by the thumb of heat" – a nice turn of phrase but inappropriate for the day!

As we came closer to Bitola the main road was closed because of subsidence and we had climb into the hills, and into the fog, on the old road made of sets. Our first stop was at the ancient city of Heraclea founded in the 4th century. Like so many Roman sites it takes some imagination to visualise what is there. However the theatre was quite clear, as was the basilica and, with even greater clarity, the piece of sculpture on one of the main avenues showing a male torso! But the highlight of the site was undoubtedly the mosaics. There were several individual pieces, for examplef a peacock, but the best was the very large single mosaic that was at least 25 feet long and 6 feet wide and in near perfect condition. It was a colourful scene telling the story of creation with flowers, trees and lots of animals. Quite beautiful.

On site there was also a little museum with some beautiful things like the glass, weights of various sizes, oil lamps and jewellery. The detail made it difficult to realise just how old they were. On the lower level a "green man" from the theatre was just like the ones we see in our old churches and a mask of Flavious in white marble was superbly executed.

The next stop was the town museum where we were supposed to look at the Atatürk rooms but we preferred the main part of the museum and was completely taken with the exhibits from pre-history to mammoths and mastodons through to modern elephants. A well laid out and easy to follow exhibition.

As we walked down the rain soaked streets we were conscious of the developing café society of Bitola though it wasn't yet sophisticated.the local farmer drove his tractor along the street, but today everyone sheltered under umbrellas or inside. It was at one of the restaurants along the pedestrian street that we had lunch; very good it was too and the green card duly appeared again

The cathedral church of St. Dimitri was built during the Ottoman period and therefore had to be plain on the outside, not drawing attention to itself but inside was a revelation. Its iconostases were fantastic displaying more than 1700 icons in a beautifully carved and huge framework. In this carving were all sorts of animals, storytelling scenes and people with amazing character in their faces. Also carved by the same craftsmen was a pulpit set high above the worshippers and accessed by a very steep little staircase. Lighting the church were the most elaborate chandeliers we have ever seen. It was quite a place.

The mosque built in 1560 was equally magnificent. It had been built using stone from the ancient city but inside it was an unusually elaborately decorated mosque with huge chandeliers. The colours, plants and rural scenes were a delight. The large central dome soared above us and appeared to be totally unsupported. Apart from those features there were all the usual things one expects to find in a mosque.It was still raining as we emerged from the mosque; the roads were awash with water and with some difficulty we braved the ridiculous traffic to cross the road to the souk where there was some shelter from the rain. It was interesting but we had seen better local markets. One plus was that there were umbrellas for sale. We should have gone to the hammam but there was a distinct lack of enthusiasm so Ace was phoned and the small van arrived, did an impressive U-turn in the horrendous traffic which allowed us to squeeze between taxis and cars and to pile in with Liz and Mike, Ingrid and Norman and Derek in the front seat. Our itinerary included going to see the French WWI cemetery which was immaculate with its carefully tended garden and rows of white crosses, all very poignant.

The run back should have been delightful through the mountains and forests but they were shrouded in rain and mist. The evening was "at leisure" but included dinner; in view of the weather we again had to go in the minibus. It was very pleasant and the company excellent.

The next day dawned grey and wet. we were relocating to Skopje, 171 km away. First stop was Struga <u>and</u> the sun was shining! It was a pleasant small town. The River Drim ran through the town and we took the opportunity to walk alongside it, over the little bridge, ignoring the sign saying "Strictly no crossing this bridge". Some of us wandered down to the lake and onto the pebble beach, deciding it held a lot of potential. We hadn't been given any specific instruction about meeting back in the bus so we were rather tardy.! As a result we were late arriving at the monastery of St. John the Baptist which stands on a hill overlooking the rolling countryside. We entered through the arch sheltered by a dome and past the wash basins and taps for the pilgrims to clean themselves before entering. On the wall above the basins was a fine icon for the faithful to meditate and to prepare themselves for worship.

The church here was first established in 1020 on the site when a miraculous icon appeared, and because of this the influence of the order once stretched as far Albania. The present church dates from the 18th and 19th centuries having been destroyed by the Ottomans three times. Even in May of this year it had suffered from another devastating fire; we could still smell the charred wood. As you walked in the interior seemed plain but then you saw the carved iconostasis. It was superb and stretched the whole width of the church and nearly to the ceiling. In it there were 500 people including a representation of the two brothers who had carved it. There were also over 200 animals; the people in traditional dress and in scenes from the old and new testaments. You could easily have spent all day looking at it and finding new things to marvel at. The same brothers also produced the bishop's seat in the church. Just in front of the iconostasis was an elaborately displayed silver icon of St. John and supposed to be the oldest in the world.

All of this history, art and craftwork is cared for by the 18monks still living and worshipping in the monastery. We saw a few of them going about their tasks in their black clerical dress and black headgear. It was a most interesting visit.

The run to Tetova was excellent through the tree covered

Struga mountains which rose on both sides of the road. The colours in the trees were just beginning to show; there were yellows, oranges, green and occasionally a vivid red. For many miles the river ran alongside us sometimes widening out into a lake. Some of these lakes were dammed as part of the hydro-electric power system. An unusual sight on the other side of one of the lakes was a massive white deposit, apparently the source of a sulphur spring. This was confirmed a minute later when the rotting egg smell reached us!

Lunch was at a rather posh hotel which involved quite a detour to reach there passing across a dam and then driving up a long winding road lined with Swiss type chalets used in the winter for skiing. The hotel was built on the side of the hill and had a magnificent restaurant with huge picture windows overlooking the river and far hills.

After lunch there was a long run to the Tekke centre belonging to the Sufi order of the Dervishes – great excitement we thought. We had long lecture from their principal on their religion. He was clearly a most devout man of high principles but he did go on a bit about their harmonious living, their equality for men and women and their generally peaceful outlook on life. They don't preach to convert people, they must wish to join the order and demonstrate that wish by good living and actions and they may then be accepted by the community.

They were most generous and courteous to us producing sweet tea, apples (tho' rather gnarled) and cake. Baba Mundi who spoke to us was a fine figure of a man in his white robes and white hat with its green band. On this band was a diamante brooch of a seahorse; this is a symbolic animal for the Sufi as it acts as mother and father to its children. (The male sea horse carries the young in his pouch till they are "born").

We eventually emerged, this time without the Sunni Muslim gentleman who had accosted us when arriving. He had been most unhappy about us going to see the Sufi who were disliked in the area and had been persecuted over the years. He tried to block our way but eventually relented. Going out we were only hindered by the wandering cows going to look for better grass!

There was a short drive to the "painted mosque". An unusual mosque because it was decorated both inside and out with glorious paintings – no people feature of course because it is against Islam to portray the human person. Outside the walls were divided into panels and were all decorated in abstract designs in blues, reds, greens and browns, many of the panels having a central roundel in a different colour. The outside hardly prepared us for the inside which was a mass of colour, of plants, flowers, painted vases and urns on every wall. In the centre was a large dome in yellow and blue surrounded by a red border and around this a set of beautiful rural scenes within round frames. The two corner galleries were also elaborately decorated.

As we entered the mosque we had of course removed our shoes and left them carefully at the side of the steps. However as we came out we got shouted at by an old Muslim; we couldn't understand what we were doing wrong after all we had taken off our shoes. The problem was as we put them on we stood on the carpet! Not allowed.

The run into Skopje was in the dark which somehow

emphasised the poverty in the town and generally in Macedonia. In the wet and dark it all looked like the developing country it is.

The Best Western Hotel really was, as promised, in the centre of town and did have comfortable good sized rooms though not the tea and coffee making as promised.

Dinner was quite special tonight; it was arranged by Mia and was at her mother's restaurant. She had apparently cooked for the UN so we had high expectations, which were met. There were a huge number of different dishes including for that strange creature "a vegetarian". We felt embarrassed by the amount we couldn't eat we were so full! At the end of the evening there was a brilliant moment when Lucy announced the engagement of Ace and Mia. Everyone was genuinely delighted and plied them with questions like when? Where? How many guests and is Lucy one of them? We had had a super day and evening.

At breakfast next day we were bemused when the waitress on duty came over to us and asked me, "Is that your husband?" I answered, "Yes." She replied, "I could tell. You looked at him with love." An interesting exchange so early in the day.

We met our dapper little guide, with the unlikely name Zoran, outside the hotel and opposite the newly built monument to Mother Theresa. From there we walked along the pedestrian street admiring the art deco buildings and the numerous sculptures by local artists as far as the 15th-century bridge built by the Ottomans, the Stone Bridge, which had survived the 1963 earthquake that razed much of Skopje. Looking down at the River Vardar from the bridge we could see a lot of construction work going on in the river,; two large fountains were being built as well as a "glass eye" bridge, a new pedestrian bridge.

Two imposing statues stood on the other side of the bridge, they were Cyril (responsible for the Cyrillic alphabet) and Methodicus. They were Byzantine brothers who did much for the development of the Slav culture. They are usually depicted with Cyril in a monastic habitand Methodicus as a bishop.

We had a gentle walk along a shopping street, in the rain, towards the mosque we were to visit as it was the only known first floor mosque. This was its only distinction; it was otherwise fairly ordinary; it didn't allow women in to the prayers at all because there were no curtains on the small gallery and therefore no way of hiding them!

The bazaar wasn't particularly noteworthy in goods, produce, colour or atmosphere. It had been destroyed in the 17th century by fire caused by oil lamps setting light the wooden shops. We walked through it to the National museum; the entrance was not imposing and in one way was quite weird. We initially stood in a weed and rubbish strewn square in front of a statue of a princess. This was really quite charming but on looking down there at her feet was a gruesome half skull complete with teeth although of animal origin. There were some interesting artefacts including beautiful 6th century crucifixes of most unusual design; but the most outstanding exhibit was of icons; they were superb and made more accessible by an elderly gentleman who followed us round explaining the significance of the features of the icon and also making sure we didn't lean too close and trigger the alarms.

A short walk took us past the Mustafa Pasha Mosque, the highly decorated largest mosque in Skopje. Unfortunately it was closed for a big renovation and construction of a fountain for the ritual cleansing before prayer.It was on then to the monastery of St. Spas (Holy Salvation); it was delightful and one of the most beautiful we saw in all Macedonia.

It was built initially in the 4th century and rebuilt during the Ottoman period when it was illegal for a Christian church to be taller than a mosque so it was built underground which allowed the original bell tower to stand but still be below the minaret. Because of its design its doors are very low, nearly everyone, especially the men have to bend low. This apparently had a dual purpose; it made all men, including Muslims bow as they entered a church and also leaves them vulnerable if they are attacking the building.

Steep steps led us to the three naves of the church where we were met by the sight of the most magnificent iconostasis. Three famous woodcarvers from the same village took five years (1819 to 1824) to complete the 10m long and 6m high iconostasis carved in walnut. It is made of two rows of partly inlaid icons of scenes from the Old and New Testaments. All the characters are dressed in traditional Macedonian costume. One of our group did spot signs of woodworm and pointed them out to the guide who explained that in fact the whole church has to be fumigated every few years to preserve the wood.

The church was situated at one corner of a courtyard in the centre of which stood a white sarcophagus. It contained the remains of a revolutionary who was the leader of Independence for Macedonia. He was beheaded in 1903 and his head was lost probably, after being stuck on the stone bridge; the rest of his body exhumed and moved to the present position in 1964.

By now it was definitely lunch time which we had in a "caravanari" an ancient stopping place for food, drink and rest by the nomadic people. Also where they came to buy and sell their animals. It was delightful, very atmospheric partly because we were squeezed into a small room with decorative brick work, arched windows and ethnic plates on the walls. We had all been saying that two large meals a day were too much so lunch was billed as just a "starter" plate and pudding. Good just what we wanted, that was until it arrived. It was a huge plate full of delicious salads, cheeses, olives, and little balls of something nice but not identifiable and meat (for those without a green card). It was accompanied by a big flat loaf also delicious. Pudding was a macaroon type pastry, passed on to my neighbour!

There was time to look round the bazaar before climbing to the Kale fortress. Excavations suggest there has been a fort since 200BC; artefacts have been found from this era. The massive earthquake in 1963 razed most of the fort. For centuries stone from previous building on the site has been re-used; for example the ramp we walked up was built from ancient Skopje destroyed in 213; the massive old town walls from the Roman city.

From the top there were splendid views of the modern city including the 20-storey radio and TV tower; the Macedonians are very proud of this building because it is 4 storeys higher than allowed by the planners who restrict the height because of the earthquake danger. We could see some of the 16 new suburbs of modern houses created after the quake. Later in the afternoon we saw more housing developments of prefabs just like we had in our country after the war. A real cause of concern for the government in the last 15 years has been that between 100,000 and 150,000 young people have emigrated to find work and education.

The minibus and van took us to the little village of Gorno Nerezi and the exquisite tiny church of Sveti Pantelejmon. The exterior was the usual lovely brickwork, tiny arched windows, low doors and small domes. Inside were more super frescoes many from the 12th century, recognisable by the brilliant cobalt blue in the fresco; others, restored after a quake in 1550, had a browner cast. The scenes were vivid and the figures interesting, according to Lucy because they were elongated showing "downfall". We were interested other frescoes; St. John at the feet of Jesus; the entry into Jerusalem; very human little boys hiding up a tree and laying clothes before Christ as he entered Jerusalem; the moving Pieta and the poignant picture of the father holding up his baby for a blessing.

Dinner ended a very good and interesting day.

Our excursion next day took us northwards towards Serbia and Kosovo. On the way we passed a number of factories which were, apparently, funded by tax breaks for foreign investors; there was an oil refinery sponsored by Greece, a British factory producing electrical components for cars and other unidentified works. In between there was rolling countryside and a flat topped, extinct volcano with a small community living and existing there because of the many stones that made building dwellings that bit easier. They survive today by quarrying and the extraction of clay for bricks.

In the distance was the hermit's cave, now a church. The hermit prophesised that a certain passing soldier would one day be emperor – he was and built the church in recognition of the wisdom of the hermit. But we were heading for the monastery church of Sveti Georgi in the tiny village of Staro Nagorichane. Another lovely stone and brick church with five domes. It was built in 1313 after a lot of political wrangling including an arranged marriage, on the base of the original church, this can still be seen. Also visible on the outside letters which represent the words of a sacred song – "light of Christ seen in us all".

The interior was a mass of frescoes (!) executed by King Milutin's famous court painters. The representations of the Last Supper were especially good; we were able to see them clearly by pulling back the curtain, which is usually firmly drawn, to stop anyone (especially women) except the priest appreciating them. The best, however, were in a little side chapel dedicated to St. Nicholas, into which we had to squeeze 2 or 3 at a time. These were of the said saint calming the waters on which they were sailing. Another one showed him cutting down a tree because it produced no fruit; this was an allegory condemning "gays" in the community. The detail and colour were superb and at least one of the subjects caused a certain amount of comment from the group.

Time then for lunch; it was quite a run to the isolated restaurant, set in countryside and displaying old agricultural artefacts. It was an unusual lunch consisting of a large bowl of a variety of beans with sausages floating on top! One lady on leaving was heard to say, in a Home Counties accent, "I suppose that was rural food." I guess it was.

The funniest incident of the trip was the reaction of Peter (a confirmed bachelor) to two young women arriving at the restaurant as we were all leaving. They were very skimpily clad, with very short skirts and very long legs; he got totally excited about them, positively jumping up and down. He must have led a sheltered life!

We returned to Skopje and were given "time off". Just outside the hotel was the memorial to Mother Theresa; a lovely statue outside the chapel dedicated to her. This was built on the site that her house had occupied. It was demolished to make room for a shopping centre! It was a strange building all odd shapes and decorated with white and blue fish shapes. Inside the museum was interesting with things from her school days, her passport and her family. On the upper floor was a simple chapel with an icon, an altar, flowers and chairs arranged for prayer.

Coming out of the chapel we walked down the main street admiring the many modern sculptures then turning left we found, eventually, the modern Orthodox Cathedral with its domes roofed in black and lined in white – quite eye catching. There was a wedding about to take place; the bride was waiting, the groom on his mobile and no bridesmaids. Soon a lady arrived clutching a bouquet – apparently the missing bridesmaid so the wedding procession could enter the church; some of the guests (a motley crew) wandered along behind including one bloke with his can of beer! They "disappeared" down the vast interior and we peeped inside. It was certainly magnificent with a huge and impressive modern iconostasis and a massive chandelier.

Mia told us that few attend the normal services, no-one sits except the very elderly and there is no singing. The priest recites the liturgy from the altar and only he takes the bread and wine. Communion is only celebrated at Easter and Christmas.

We returned via the wine festival that was going on near the Stone Bridge; it was lively even in the afternoon and more so later in the evening. As we passed the memorial to Mother Theresa we were intrigued by the group of nuns in the blue and white habit of her order. They were disappointed not to be able to get into the chapel which had just closed.

Just near the memorial house we were intrigued by a very large poster of a young man that had been erected in the garden and that was surrounded by candles. We enquired of a young woman, who was giving the candles to passers-by, who he was; she told us he was a famous, popular and successful Macedonian singer and also a great humanitarian who had done a great deal for the deprived and homeless young people. He had been killed in an accident a year ago.

We got ready for dinner which we actually walked to.

We now came to our last full day. We set off to the north of Skopje passing a huge cemetery with the graves carefully tended and covered in flowers. The church itself was a pretty building set in its own grounds, built in1594. Just outside the church was a splendid store of logs for the still working oven. The frescoes had to be painted between April and October because the weather conditions were right at that time. The higher level of frescoes was painted by the pupils of the school and they also helped to mix the colours and paint the bodies or costumes of other subjects but the master did the faces. Today some of the frescoes are damaged; others in a poor condition but overall there were some delightful scenes including the saints depicted in armour because the church was originally built to celebrate war victories. The second and third zones are covered with Christ's suffering, the road to Golgotha and the crucifixion. At this time there was a strong cult of the Virgin who was believed to intercede between us and God, so she appears in very many frescoes. All the people in the frescoes, including the Virgin were very human like part of the so called "humanising" of the Holy family. was an interesting journey. We drove over ancient cobbled roads laid in Roman times; tiny country lanes and villages with a mix of housing, some small and white surrounded by productive gardens with lots of cabbages, hens and an occasional goat; the house with extensive polytunnels growing strawberries by the hydroponic method; but also dwellings that can only be described as hovels.

We were soon going through a gorge lined by high towering rocks and mountains. The sides were lined by trees in various hues of autumn colours. Looking way down from the van windows we could glimpse canoes on the river. The van soon got as far as he could go and dropped us off to carry on, on foot. It was delightful, not too cold and even a hint of sun as we walked on the narrow path, through tunnels cut in the rock and with super views all round us. We passed the towering dam which held back the River Treska and created the man-made lake.

We stopped at a point where the next church was to be visited as well as a welcome loo stop and a restaurant, our lunch beckoned, but first the church; dedicated to St. Andrew and from 1388. It was a tiny beautiful church with the Dormition of Mary above the west window; the Annunciation in the apse and the other usual subjects though they all seemed to be in miniature they were so small but still intricate in detail and beautiful colours. One amusing incident was when the local guide referred to "a laminated Jesus" (rather than the *lamentation* of Jesus.)

Lunch proved unusual and good, although a bit chilly. We were outside under the permanent awning, round several big tables. When it arrived it came with a flourish <u>each</u> of us had a large round loaf, the centre of which was filled with delicious buttery leeks. Then along came a small tray of side dishes, sliced, marinated aubergines, spicy tomato and chilli relish, delicious cheese and yogurt. This was followed by plates of tiny cakes and coffee. One of the best lunches of the trip.

It set us up for the next excursion – a boat trip. We were issued with life jackets (we wondered if this was an unusual) and clambered perilously (reason for life jackets?) into the boats and set off up the river. It was so peaceful as we glided along with the gorge, under trees and a <u>blue</u> sky above and sun! On one side there were wooden summer houses on the bank wherever a tiny bit of land allowed building, though access was only by boat. On the other bank there was just room for the path that ran all the way along the river/lake. It was delightful and much enjoyed even though we didn't see the famous vultures or the eagles, in fact we saw no birds at all even when we stopped and experienced the complete silence of the area.

Back at the hotel there was packing to do and more

onerously, sorting out the remaining denar for books, laundry and tips and making up the shortfall with dollars and euros! Tomorrow we leave Macedonia.

Today we went to the airport via a war cemetery and a monastery. All packed, breakfasted, cases in the van's pod, we were settled in to our seats when a call went up. "Everyone got their passports? There's two left in reception!" And whose were they? Ours. How lucky that was, we could have been at the airport before we discovered our loss! So onward through some of the poorer areas of the countryside; poor housing, a lot of rubbish, derelict factories and then alongside this rather nice opulent houses complete with balconies. Our first destination was the Markov Monastery

The church was built in the 14th century and painted 30 years after its completion. It is set in a pleasant wooded valley and we entered through a small gate, with a fierce sounding guard dog, in a kennel, off to our left. Once again, there was a pretty church and over its entrance dome a beautiful fresco of St. Demetrius mounted on his white horse. Inside more super and unique frescoes in a remarkably good condition, and with still vibrant colours. In the grounds there was a bell tower, a working well and a retreat house run by the nuns who we caught a glimpse of as they scuttled quietly along the balcony leading to the dormitory or down the steps to a dining room. A male caretaker opened up the tiny museum with its few icons and silverware and then the shop with its tatty cards and little else.

At the end of this visit comments were heard along the

lines of "Beautiful, but I think I'm frescoed out." And "I've got fresco neck!" But onward to a WWI British cemetery near to Skopje. This was quite unlike any other war cemetery we'd been to. It was created after the Armistice when the burials from the Kumanovo British cemetery and the French cemeteries were all gathered together and 124 commonwealth servicemen were buried or commemorated in this one cemetery. There are 6 unidentified special memorials to 6 servicemen who are buried in a German cemetery but they have never been found. There were no white crosses here just flat stones marking the grave and with moving inscriptions – "Private Cruikshank RASC who died aged 33 from his loving wife and two little sons. Not lost but gone before."

We were all a bit subdued after this visit but the mood was lightened when it was decided we would give Mia, Alex and John the driver their Thank You envelopes. The next stop would be the airport where time is tight and the main focus of the party changes. They were received with thanks and they then said they had "goody" bags for us – one per couple and one for each single passenger. They were most interesting with fridge magnets, a CD of photos of the trip and homemade cookies from Mia's mother.

So to the airport and for the first time we encountered a traffic jam near to the unfinished university! Goodbyes were said, cases claimed and then checked in, we had an invitation to the "lounge" where we got a snack to keep us going. We were entertained by the long legged blonde who insisted she had a business class ticket but it wasn't on her boarding card, therefore, she couldn't have the lounge. After a lot of to-ing and fro-ing she stayed in the lounge but then started the next dispute; her bags would have to be offloaded as they were in the wrong baggage area, she was, to put it mildly, cross. We never heard the end on the saga because her flight to Istanbul was called. Soon after ours was also called; we were two of the three in business where we had a very nice male steward with lots of "sparkling" wine and a reasonable meal.

Chapter 3
Malaysia: Deep jungle and skyscraper hotels

In 1986 neither of us had travelled in the far east when out of the blue came an invitation that changed all that. At the time I was Chief Examiner for a Diploma in Personnel Management run by the British Institute of Personnel Management (now the Chartered Institute of Personnel and Development). I had been invited by the Malaysian Institute of Personnel Management to visit Kuala Lumpur to help inaugurate a Diploma in Personnel Management closely modelled on that run by IPM in the UK with some variations to suit local circumstances.

Arrangements were made for me to travel and stay for 10 days of consultation and teaching of an initial group of 25 students. There was a small problem as there was a change on 24th December in my flight which was altered from 28th December to 26th.When I arrived at the airport in Kuala Lumpur there was no-one to meet me, as the MIPM office had been closed over the Christmas/New year period, so I took a taxi to the hotel, where I knew I was booked.

As we drove I noticed several road signs with the symbol AWAS and asked the driver what it meant, to which he replied, with a sly grin," Asian women are sexy," so that was my introduction to the far east.

That was the first of many visits to KL later when Barbara was able to join me as we went beyond KL to Sarawak, Sabah, Thailand, Vietnam, Cambodia, and Singapore, but first to Malaysia.

Malaysia

Malaysia is a combination of two territories: West (Peninsular) Malaysia) and East Malaysia on the island of Borneo, 450 miles away across the South China Sea, comprising Sabah and Sarawak.

After unsuccessful attempts at colonisation by the Portuguese and the Dutch, the British arrived in 1824, having already established trading posts at Penang and Singapore. By 1930 had established control of all three into the Crown Colony of the Malay Straits covering the whole of the Malay peninsula. During WW2 the Japanese overran the whole of Malaysia, Singapore and Thailand until the war ended in 1946. Malaysia claimed independence in 1957, but Singapore, split off in 1959.

Malaysia's capital is Kuala Lumpur stands at the confluence of the Kelang and Gombak rivers 19 miles inland from the straits of Malacca; the name comes from Malay words which translate as" Muddy River Mouth". It was originally a mining camp, which grew rapidly to become the economic centre of Selangor State, the most highly developed in the country with it's fair share of skyscrapers and plush hotels one of which the Petaling Jaya Hilton was usually our berth when in KL. The most spectacular building is the Petronas Towers which is an office block surmounted by two towers 1,250 feet tall, named after the Petronas oil company who paid for it. Quite a lot of companies were drilling for oil sea, and this leads on to a slightly amusing story: Barbara and I were staying in our usual hotel in KL, where after doing my stint with MIPM I had agreed to do an overnight trip to a drilling site off the coastal town of Miri where I would give a talk on performance-related pay. Barbara, being a biologist decided she would take an overnight trip into Taman Negara a National Park at the centre of the jungle.

Barbara was collected by the tour operator and I was driven to the airport by our local "minder" a very attractive young woman allocated to us to take us wherever e needed to go; in this case it was the airport for the short flight to Miri. On arrival I was taken to the shore base which was a quite lavish sort of country club on the beach with the rig visible in the distance. My room was very comfortable and I enjoyed an excellent lunch with the company personnel manager before delivering my talk and engaging in a lively question and answer session which afterwards continued on the beach on one end if which there were half a dozen WAGS who were accompanying their husbands and taking the opportunity to study for qualifications by correspondence.They appeared to be holding their own seminar.

I was driven to the airport, flew back to KL to be collected by our minder who drove to the hotel, where she ordered a pot of tea with cakes for two in the lounge. We engaged in polite conversation until Barbara returned, having been dropped off by her tour operator. She went to reception and asked, "Has my husband returned yet?" The receptionist, knowing that I was in the lounge, having tea with a young woman, said, "No, not yet." – following the practice of telling the customer what she would like to hear, even if not accurate. Barbara's reply was, "Never mind, just give me the key and I'll go up to the room." "No, sorry. Room not ready." Our minder heard this exchange and went to fetch her, to avoid any further complications.

Now we move to East Malaysia where a few years later we travelled independently to Sabah, the easternmost point of the country, traditionally known as "the land below the wind" from the days of sail. We based ourselves at the Tanjung Aru resort, which was absolutely splendid with beaches and considerable comfort, from which you could explore the local towns and villages and further afield was the sepilok reserve, where baby orang utans are rescued and prepared to return to the wild after having been kept as pets in families.

They are very attractive to children when young, but when they grow to a full size arboreal ape, they are obviously unmanageable and too often they are discarded before reaching that stage. We found our visit quite fascinating. Nearby there were bat caves; nothing to do with Batman of popular culture but huge caves where bats live and breed so that they can be used to make such eastern delicacies as bird's nest soup.

Thailand

Bangkok is the capital of Thailand, previously Siam. Many people will have seen the play or film, "Anna and the King of Siam" in which Deborah Kerr played the part of a Victorian governess in hooped skirts opposite Yul Brynner as a 19th-century King of Siam who had engaged Anna to tutor his many children in English. is subtle

His subtle diplomacy had saved his country from European colonisation, unlike other countries in South East Asia; now western tourists flock to see this oriental gem.

Our journey was in two stages, starting on a very hot day in Cheshire, we went to Manchester airport to take an Emirates flight to Dubai, which was excellent with very good food. At Dubai we went into the Duty free which was amazing with all manner of goods on display including a Porshe saloon car. It was like a small brightly lit village with throngs of people milling around, even at 1.30 a.m.

After our initial wander around we moved into the lounge to wait for our flight to Bangkok, so we were able to doze, eat some excellent food and read until our flight was called. It was again a very good flight with a very pleasant stewardess. On our arrival in Bangkok we were met by a representative of our travel agent, Diethelm, who drove us, very slowly through an endless traffic jam to The Imperial Hotel that was grand in an old-fashioned way. Our room was excellent and there was time for a swim in the pool before dinner in the hotel. Finally we strolled to the Erawan Shrine, a popular meeting place where we were able to by Hagan Daz ice cream for the walk back.

The mext day we set off to walk to Jim Thompson's house. Jim Thompson was an American architect, who served in the military during WW2 and was a military intelligence officer as part of the force that liberated Thailand. Enchanted by the country, he returned when the war was over and adopted Thailand as his permanent residence. he realised that there was a neglected cottage industry in the hand weaving of silk cloth. He invigorated the industry and contributed substantially to the world-wide reputation of Thai silk.

Being a trained architect, he had his home built to traditional Thai design of elevating the house by a full storey above the ground to avoid flooding in the rainy season. As it was a Buddhist holiday recognising the death of the King's mother, the house was closed, but we could look around the outside, a very interesting trip.

Later we crossed the river by Long tail boat to visit Wat Arun, Temple of the Dawn. It is so impressive that Barbara decides to climb to the second level up very steep steps! Then we hail a Tuk Tuk to return to the Imperial for lunch and a rest before the evening of traditional Thai meal and Dance. We are collected by minibus with Bernie from Florida and Mona from Tunisia(who Bernie took a shine to) and two East German girls, and we go to Silom village with very attractive shops and eating places as well as a hall that is packed with tourists. After the traditional Thai meal we see some wonderfully graceful dancing in traditional costumes. Then back to the hotel, with the prospect of a very early start tomorrow.

We're up early as we're going in a short trip for a few days up country and we start by being collected in a Range rover type of vehicle and then transferred to a coach which takes us on a pleasant drive through the countryside of paddy fields until we arrived at the WW2 museum showing the deprivations suffered by British and Australian prisoners of War made to work on the Thailand to Burma railway near the   town of Kanchanaburi, where we also see the cemetery of the allied troops who died in the process. Then we moved to the actual section of the bridge itself that they had built before liberation..It was built from timber at a cost of many lives.

A great film, "Bridge over the River Kwai" was made in 1957 starring Alec Guinness, which presented a vivid picture of the brutality of the Japanese in their attempts to drive a rail connection through Burma to India. Our visit was a chilling experience. In contrast our overnight stay was in the River Kwai Village Hotel was delightful, as we had a deluxe suite with a balcony from which we could see the river trickling quietly by through unspoilt jungle scenery with kingfishers and water buffalo in the distance.

We had a very good dinner in the hotel including a vegetarian meal with lots of bean curd for Barbara, all followed by a display of dancing by a group of little girls who were daughters of people who worked at the resort. They were totally unsophisticated and quite charming.....and so to bed.

The next day we were collected and returned to Bangkok and met Mr Booi, our guide and Mr Suk to start our drive to Ayudhya, a former capital of Thailand, where we saw three huge bronze Buddhas, original black, now gold with mother of pearl eyes. We also saw historical park with royal palaces.

Further on we visit the PhraBuddha with it's shrine of the holy footprint of Lord Buddha and the nearby monkey temple. Finally we proceed to the Pailyn Sukhotai Hotel for dinner and overnight stay. The following morning after breakfast we set off for Sukhotai, the first capital of Thailand from 1257 to 1379. We see various wats including Maha Dahat, Sr sri cum and return to Sukothai hotel for dinner and overnight.at the same hotel.

The next morning we are late in leaving as there is a dispute about the bill which the tour company has to pay, but MrBooi eventually sorts it out and we are off to Chiang Mai. Early in the Journey we stop at Mr Booi's family house, which is fascinating. It is all one room with a teak floor and no furniture..There is a t..v, a video, a washing machine and rolled-up bedrolls as well as a baby's hammock and an (ancient) mother in law of 74 years. The family business was trading in teak wood and teak furniture.;garlic, and small onions were sold in the local market. A family rice field was rented out.

Before leaving we drank some coconut milk from the tree outside the house, and it tasted like a young coconut. Taking our leave ofthefamily, we went into the village to shop for thai apples, longons, rambutan and mangustein. Several ladies had buckets holding items for sale such as flowers, food and air letters, whichwere pre-printed letters into which you placed yor message for those who had passed on to the afterlife and posted it. Next was.lunch in a large airy restaurant with lots of fans.

Finally our journey ended at Chiang Mai, a town near the frontier with Burma. We hit the rush hour, but apparently it is always rush hour. The Amari Rincome hotel was to be our billet, which was very nice indeed. We had a splendid room overlooking the pool and the beautiful gardens as well as the mountains in the distance. We were tempted to have our dinner in their French restaurant but eventually settled for the coffee shop with it's more varied menu.

Next morning we booked a tour of the night bazaar. we were picked up in a minibus which took us down to the centre and let us loose for an hour, so we wandered happily among flowers and fruits and masses of umbrellas from a local factory and then had difficulty finding the car park where the minibus was waiting. the following day we had a tour to an elephant camp where elephants are trained for moving large amounts of teak and Barbara enjoyed sitting for a few minutes on an elephant's coiled trunk.. We also went to an orchid farm with some gorgeous blooms and a small butterfly farm.

We moved next to a white karen hill tribe village with a very primitive way of life in that very young girls have a brass ring fitted round their necks, and it remains there for the rest of their lives with an additional ring being fitted for each year of their lives. You can imagine what a barbaric practice this was as the neck was steadily lengthened putting pressure on the clavicle and compressing the rib cage. as well as the physical harm, pain and discomfort, the women are a tourist attraction as people like ourselves visit the village solely to stare at them and take photographs (although we didn't), but we were rather ashamed at patronising a freak show.

The next day we were transferred to the local airport for the short flight to Mae Hong sorn where were collected by_the minibus of or hotel, the Tara, where we had a very welcome drink while registering. It was a delightful 4-star hotel in a superb location with great views into Burma (recently known as Myanmar).After lunch we took the hotel bus down to the centre of town, which was a super unspoilt rural town where we bought a wood carving, drinks, fruit and took the bus back. At dinner in the hotel we were intrigued by our fellow diner; one family group of three Danes, father, son and mother, who always walked in single file and in that order, an American family of Dad, Mom and three kids; four brits - mum, dad, son and daughter.

Next day the alarm went at 6.30 so that we were able to have an early breakfast and take the hotel minibus into town for the early market, where we saw monks receiving rice and hundreds of local residents buying fruit, flowers, indescribable meats and rice. We bought ear rings, a lacquered box and an elephant bell. We found a tuk tuk to take us back to the hotel just as it started to rain heavily, and kept on raining for a very long time, proving that the tuk tuk is not an ideal vehicle for a thunderstorm. the evening buffet at the hotel was excellent and the hotel was filling up.

Next morning it was still raining and we had nothing to do until our transfer to the airport at 11.30. when we got to the airport we heard that our aircraft had made two attempts to land, but the cloud was too low and it was returning to Chiang Mai for the night with a view to making a third attempt the next day, so it was back to the hotel for us until tomorrow.

next day we were loaded onto the aircraft and then unloaded as the air conditioning was not working; then re loaded only to be unloaded again as one of the engines was not working properly. There was a degree of tension in the departure lounge, but eventually we were re-loaded again and we were on our way to Singapore on what was a good flight with a very good meal!

For us it was a fleeting visit to see the Royal Palace, which was a miracle of gold and bright colours, and then on the see the Golden Buddha, a huge gilded figure lying on his side in a custom-built building.

Part Two

Mainly by train

Chapter 4
India: Touring Rajahstan on the Toy Train and the Palace on Wheels

This was our second trip to India, the first was on part of a cruise, but this time we we travelled with a company called Great Train Journeys. First we flew down to Heathrow and then with Virgin, so we transferred to the Virgin Club, which was superb, with bars, a deli, a full service restaurant, champagne bar, a beauty spa and a film theatre. Sadly Barbara could do no more than sleep,having been afflicted with a virus of some sort. we set off soon towards India in late afternoon. The service and food were excellent, although barbara could only manage a dry biscuit and a glass of bubbly, her special medicine. The bed was even better and we slept most of the flight, waking up in time for breakfast. We had arrived in Delhi!

Delhi is actually two cities: Old Delhi is a walled city of narrow bustling streets, enlived by lots of small businesses doing brisk businesses doing brisk trade. It is centred on the Red Fort, built by the same Sha Jahan as were to visit much later in our trip. Getting off the plane we were hit by the Indian heat, which would follow us for the next fortnight.The terminal was in Old Delhi and we were aghast at the mass of exposed electric cables, ceilings lacking tiles, but very nice marble floors. The cases arrived and were loaded into the coach and we were off to our hotel. Initially it was through a mass of people and vehicles. New Delhi, however, built for the British by Sir Edward Lutyens in 1911, although it was not fully functioning until 1931.The roads changed from narrow and crowded to wide, tree-lined boulevards. The contrast is amazing

The Claridges is an elegant hotel standing in its own green gardens. We were greeted by a splendid uniformed doorman who always opened the door for us no matter how often, and how quickly we went through. There was a pleasant reception, a welcome drink served in the sitting room, which was conveniently surrounded by up market shops, especially attractive to the shopaholics among us. Everything looked promising. our room keys were handed out and we st off for Room 11 on the ground floor and convenient for the restaurant. It did, however, seem rather dark and when we drew back the curtains there was a very large panel obscuring the hotel car park. On entering the bathroom we found a shower with a seat and safety rails but no cubicle to prevent the rest of the room getting wet. It. was a disabled room in several senses of the word.. We mentioned it to our tour manager, Ian, as e realised that someone had to have that room, But we did not want it when we returned to the hotel later before returning home.

We had a snack lunch in the gardens and remained there for a pleasant afternoon despite the traffic outside and the cacophony of horns that Indians find impossible not to use permanently.

The bird life was interesting despite the urban setting..

Black kites wheeled overhead, Parakeets screeched in the trees and starling - like birds foraged on the lawn

Dinner was a very nice buffet, although Barbara didn't do it justice. We sat with Mark and Cheryl from the New Forest, and we were intrigued to hear how they had sold up in the West Country and bought an ex-army tin hut and its large plot of land. Then they set about building their own large house from scratch, from books, while they lived in a caravan!

Next morning we were off to see the sights of Delhi, first by driving along impressive wide roads to India Gate, an impressive sandstone monument by Lutyens, that was uncannily like the Arc de Triomphe in Paris. It was built to honour the soldiers who died in WW1 and the Afghan war in 1919. Framed in the arch is a stone canopy, also by Lutyens, where originally stood a statue of George V in Imperial robes. After India's independence in 1947 it was removed.

Our next stop was Raj Gat, where Gandhi was cremated after his assassination. After removing our shoes and avoiding the extremely hot paving, we went into the peaceful, pleasant gardens surrounding the simple black platform with an eternal flame and garlands of orange marigolds to commemorate Gandhi. Surrounding the gardens was a high bank with a walkway on top, where we were surprised to see armed soldiers. We soon saw why, as a long line of chanting orange-clad monks began to emerge and congregate by the memorial. some were holding photographs of the Dalai Lama, and we learned that they were part of a group of 250 who were marching from northern Delhi back to Tibet. It was all part of a demonstration that had followed the progress of the Olympic flame around the world protesting against the Chinese treatment of many of its citizens, especially the Tibetans, as Beijing was hosting the Olympic games that year. The torch had passed through Delhi yesterday. No-one was allowed near to see it after troubles in London, Paris and in America.

The monks were charming and did not mind being photographed, even when, what a chanting their prayers. Somehow it was quite a special moment.

Then it was back on the coach to Old Delhi, what a contrast! Originally it was a walled city though few remnants of these walls remain. The streets in the Old City are chaotic: narrow, crowded and people selling everything you could possibly want, from car doors, bicycles, fruit live hens, as well as the butchers with garish displays of meat, as well as cobblers, barbers, scooters and rickshaws. Electricity came late to the city and masses of cables run just above the heads of the people with junctions like bowls overflowing with spaghetti. There were so many people of all ages, sizes and occupations carrying out every manner of job or task.

Our destination was the Friday mosque, Jama Masjid, the largest mosque in India able to accommodate 25,000 in worship. Visitors are admitted until noon, so we had to hurry as the time was approaching, but we still had to remove our shoes and be modestly dressed. This involved some of our party, both men and women, wearing long cloths as skirts or to cover their shoulders. The lack of shoes meant that you had to walk round the vast courtyard with care as any part of it not covered by carpet or hessian was far too hot to tread on. We made our way round the edge of the courtyard to where the families were seated, waiting for Friday prayers. t seemed to be a happy, convivial time; the children were playing, the women gossiping among themselves, and the men, sitting apart from the family, putting the world to rights.

As unbelievers we couldn't go into the mosque itself, but at one corner there was a tall red brick minaret which we could see from the outside;   On the north western side there was a small shed-like building which supposedly housed a hair from the Prophet, a sandal and a footprint. Our guide was getting agitated that we were still in the mosque as noon was imminent, so we collected our shoes and were whisked off to Broadway apparently a famous restaurant in Delhi, although the district looked rather dubious. Inside it was quite dark and dimly lit, with photographs on the walls of old film stars who had visited in some bygone era, and at the far end stood a large old Bentley. We sat at a long table with four others from our party. Lunch started with poppadoms, followed by tandoori chicken, chicken curry, lamb curry and paneer, a version of cottage cheese. This was all to western taste and was to become a part of every meal. Pudding consisted of little balls like dumplings surrounded by a sweet fruity covering, which was very nice.

After lunch we drove back into New Delhi to Rajpath, a magnificent wide road lined with trees that shaded the footpaths leading to a huge roundabout with a fine floral display and surrounding more if Lutyens buildings including the Viceroy's residence, on each side of which are equally impressive secretariat buildings.

Then it was to a more historical site, Humayun's tomb, a lovely building, said to be "Delhi's Taj Mahal". It was built in 1570 to house the tombs of various members of Indian royal families. The construction was supervised by Humayun's second wife who camped on site throughout the nine years it took to build. It really was a splendid building of red sandstone sitting on a red sandstone platform, down the centre of which ran a water-filled canal. t was inlaid with black and white marble, he first of this type and size in India. Inside the octagonal chamber stood the tomb of Humayun, a plain white sarcophagus on a simple platform.

At this point, a few words about the Mughal dynasty: they were a Muslim dynasty who invaded India in 1526, ruling the country until the early 19th century. Despite speaking Persian and being Muslims, they encouraged racial and religious harmony, developed systems of administrative efficiency as a basis for conciliating their more numerousHindu subjects and developed a distinctive style of architecture that can be seen today in Rajahstan, especially inDelhi and Agra. heir rule slowly weakened by the beginning of the 18th century. There were Hindu uprisings; Britain and France fought for supremacy across India and the British East India indu uprisings Company captured DelhiNDU SUBJECTSHI.

After our guide (JK) had finished his explanations to us we had some free time before we made our final stop at the Qutb Minar complex which is principally a 240 foot tall tower with some surrounding buildings. it marks the site of the first Muslim kingdom in northern India, and was built to celebrate the victory of IIslam over infidels in1199.India's first mosque stands next to the tower; it was built from the remains of 27 Hindu and Jain temples that were ransacked by Muslim armies. We wandered round this most interesting site watching the setting sun, and took a final look at another remarkable pillar, much smaller, but no less intriguing. made of iron and dating from the 4th century,it was originally a flagstaff and has no rust at all. It must be made of an exceptionally pure metal, but even today metallurgists can not explain how it's made.

We returned to our hotel for dinner, and so our first full day in Delhi finished. We had to be up early in the morning, so we retired to bed. It had been a fascinating, hot introduction to India, and next day we're going to Shimla.

It was certainly an early start, with the alarm going at 5.30. We just had time for a cup of tea before collecting our breakfast box and climbing aboard our coach for the journey across Delhi. Arriving near to, but not at,the railway station all our preconceptions of India were justified. to say it was chaos was no exaggeration. There was a mass of cars, aggressive taxis, tuc tucs, pedestrians and cyclists. Red-coated porters rushed across the road as soon as they spotted our tourist coach. We got down from the coach with warnings to beware of pickpockets, porters and hawkers

Luckily we did not have cases, as these were being taken to Shimla by van. We were shepherded across the road by several minders and eventually made it to Platform 1 where the Shatabdi express was waiting. It was the longest train we had ever seen; we had to find Executive Coach 2, Seats 37 and 38. We found them easily and they were excellent, with lots of room and tables on the back of the seat in front for food, crosswords and even scrabble. he train left on time, but even before the train was moving a man appeared with tea and some less welcome Indian snacks. We decided it was time to eat our breakfast from the hotel: cheese sandwiches, hard-boiled eggs, odd sausage rolls, cake, fruit and biscuits. some was eaten, some saved for later, but there was certainly enough. Then the train breakfast arrived with bowls of Kellog's cornflakes, but it was different having them with hot milk, and we could not manage the omelettes.

Replete, we settled back to watch the fascinating countryside and life on he platforms as we passed by.Much of the landscape was flat with vast fields growing cereals, where ancient tractors were working and, in some places, equally ancient harvesters. In the smaller fields all the crop was being harvested by sickle and winnowed by hand by the women. here were huge piles of grain in the fields left to dry in the sun. The only animals we saw in this region were those attached to a farmstead, a single cow or bullock; a few goats and hens.

The homes were simple concrete one room dwellings with a little cultivated area around them. These were palaces compared to the appalling conditions we saw near the bigger stations where whole families lived at the edge of the line, under cardboard or plastic sheeting, with no electricity, drainage or running water. The worst we saw were those huddled under the pylons in equally squalid conditions. We arrived at the junction of Kalka and changed platforms for Shimla and here was a long,wearying delay as the small-engine, narrow gauge locomotive needed to pull us up to Shimla had broken down, and no-one could be found to fix it.

There are several toy trains in India on the foothills of mountain ranges. Collectively they are a World Heritage site. There is an intriguing story about how they came to be built. In the late 1800s Franklin Prestage was an executive with the Eastern Bengal Railway and one evening he was at a reception with his wife. When they got up to dance Mrs Prestage complained that he was always going forward when he should be going back. This gave Franklin the idea that it might be possible for a train to go uphill by going sideways; the zig zag with hairpin bends was born and the toy train t0 Shimla was opened in 1903.

It was 60 miles to Shimla with 103 tunnels and 864 bridges. It was a triumph of British engineering, all because Franklin was a poor dancer; well done and bravely borne Mrs Prestage. At the time the only alternative was a pony and cart or hiking. The railway brought a boom to the British Raj when it moved there to avoid the summer heat of Delhi. Families could join their husbands and a colony soon developed, not only for the British but also for the many Indians needed, and still needed, to run the railway. Being a railwayman was a top job and some of them adopted an anglicised form of their name which could be inherited by their children. This continues; in the 1970s, for instance, Lancashire had a player, Farokh Engineer, who had previously played for India.

After a 90-minute wait the repaired locomotive arrived and was connected to it's carriages, a process watched with great interest by the train buffs in our party, the cows were moved off the track and with a toot we were off. It was a long journey and the line to Shimla is single track with one two points where it widens to allow trains going up can pass those waiting to go down. At least the waits gave us the chance to stretch our legs. Carriages were really small, including the plastic seats which were not that comfortable in the heat of India, and the only fresh air came from open doors. We were lucky being near the door, with extra leg room and a spare seat opposite except when our tour manager Ian sat there while visiting his flock. As we left one stop we suddenly realised that Henry was not with us, although his wife Brenda seemed unconcerned. There was much shouting for Henry to put his head out of the window if he was in the adjoining carriage: no head appeared so Ian got in touch with the support car that was tracking us by road, and asked them to return to the last stop to see if he was stranded there. He wasn't there either, but he was seen gettingout of another carriage having had a pleasant half hour in the company of Indian and other travellers who had "made me most welcome."

At another stop we nearly left behind a number of ladies who had got off to use the facilities, but they were not quick enough so the train had o slow down to get them all on. One of them was Henry's wife Brenda.

It was time to eat the packed lunches provided: sandwiches, cakes, fruit and drinks, all of which were fine but there was really too much so the children waiting at the end of the line did rather well. The journey had been fantastic despite the heat and the plastic seats. Once we had pulled out of Kalka we were in the country of rolling hills and terracing with density of cultivation even at the end of the dry season was lush, colourful and interesting, pink and red bougainvillea, bright red flowers that we couldn't identify and wonderful purple flowers on the lower slopes than, again, we couldn't identify but were most impressive. We saw a lot of Indian rural life: the planting, the harvesting, the digging by hand as well as by horse – or ox -pulled ploughs. It often seemed to us to be the women who were out in the heat working while the men were either under the trees or not to be seen at all.

We finally arrived at Shimla. Even though we had thoroughly enjoyed the ride, we were glad to be off the train. Waiting for us on the platform was a fleet of 4x4 vehicles which took us to the Oberoi Cecil hotel for the next three nights. We were very impressed by the hotel, which was a really elegant building, both inside and out and typifying the grace of the British in the Hill stations to which they retreated in the summer and from which they ruled India. The hotel stood high on the hill of Shimla, with its distinctive green pointed roof above a white facade.Inside the rooms were all set around a magnificent atrium which rose several floors to the glass roof that let in the sunshine. Each floor had a balcony running all the way round with a beautiful light wood and wrought iron balustrade. It was a delight to the eye. he bedrooms were of the same standard¨ nice size big beds, a desk, table and chairs, all set off by a view across the hills and the train track on which we had arrived.

Dinner was an excellent buffet with a mixture of western and Indian dishes, something for every one.

Some notes about the British in India. English merchants established the East India Company in 1600, having received a royal warrant to do so for the purpose of of peaceful trade. The Company grew steadily and many of the local Indian rulers allowed it to set up trading posts widely in India. Then Charles II made a judicious marriage with Catherine de Braganza of Portugal who brought a dowry including several significant parts of India.

By the 18th century, England (now Britain, since the 1707 Act of Union with Scotland) was the dominant European power and the Mughal empire was collapsing. It was no longer just peaceful trade, but full blown colonial expansion, which succeeded for a long time. There was religious tolerance, a British system of administration and good jobs in the concomitant civil service, a large army and careful conciliation of the upper classes, who were keen to learn English and for their sons to go to British public schools. Some of them were given the title of Rajah or Nawab at the same time as most of their powers were removed.

The closeness of Britain and India at the upper class level before independence is illustrated by the fact that three Indian aristocrats, K.S. Ranjitsinhji in the 1890s, K.S. Duleepsinjhi and the Nawab of Pataudi, both in the 1930s all played cricket for England. Pataudi returned in1946 as captain of the first Indian team to play cricket in England. By the middle of the 19th century a move to be independent from Britain was beginning, but it was a hundred years before it became a reality.

In 1942 Winston Churchill said in the House of Commons, "I have not become the King's First Minister in order to preside over the liquidation of the British Empire." (of which India was the jewel). Three years later he had been succeeded by Clement

Atlee, who regarded independence as a priority. It was rushed and hopelessly mismanaged. Gandhi was one of many who believed that India should remain a united country, but a Muslim lawyer and political leader could not agree the constitutional changes that would secure the rights of the Muslim minority, so the country was divided by British civil servants with catastrophic results. The division caused mayhem, resulting in war between the two countries and millions of refugees crossing the border, having found themselves arbitrarily placed in the "wrong" country amidst extensive bloodshed.

In many ways the British raj was good for India for 300 years, all spoiled by our hasty ignominious departure. The civil administration remains largely unaltered, as is the justice system and military organisation, to say nothing of the game of cricket, unquestionably the most popular sport in the country, the world's largest democracy.

Reverting to Shimla, our next day is for acclimatisation we set off in a convoy of jeeps to the viceregal lodge, home of the viceroy in the days of British rule. It was a most imposing grey stone building built in 188 and surrounded by immaculately kept gardens. It was just like a gothic baronial manor that had been moved here from Scotland. It had a splendid position on top of Observatory Hill. he Lodge now belongs to the government and houses the Indian Institute of Advanced Studies.

All students are post doctoral and carefully selected by a commitee of eminent scholars after they have submitted a precis of their proposed research topic A maximum of 40 students can be accommodated at any one time. At the time of our tour, 30 were living and working in these rather grand premises.

Soon it was time to board the jeeps again and set off along a winding road to lunch at Clarke's restaurant (an appropriate name as Barbara's maiden name was Clarke. It was a pleasant mock Tudor hotel with excellent views across Shimla and to our hotel. The food was good and we were served by extravagantly dressed waiters. After lunch we wandered outside and met an Indian family whose little girl shyly practised her English on us. The rest of our group gradually emerged from lunch and we made our way up the hill to the cream coloured red roofed Christ Church. This dominates the Ridge and was the first church built in India in 1846. It could easily fit in any English town. It was a pretty light church, painted white and with fine stained-glass windows. a fresco around the chancel window was painted by Rudyard Kipling's father. On the walls were various plaques commemorating the great and good of Shimla. There were headmistresses, school matrons, those fallen in battle and bizarrely a soldier who had been killed by the accidental discharge of his own rifle

We came out of the church into the square at the top of The Ridge which is a popular meeting place, and there were a lot of people strolling in small groups that Sunday afternoon, riding horses, selling helium balloons or clockwork toys, all making a lively, colourful pageant of people

We walked along The Ridge and on to the Upper Mall and passed theGaety theatre, currently being restored, and the half timbered post office and town Hall, both looking very English. The highest point of the Mall is Scandal point; the scandal refers to the abduction from here of the Government Official's daughter by the infatuated Singh of Patialia, who sw abduction as the only way to win his lady as permission from her father was out of he question. Standing on guard at the point were two policemen in extraordinary uniform of navy trousers, white shirts with navy and yellow braid and wide belts in the same colours. Headgear was n army - like cap set at a jaunty angle, topped by a fan-like structure also in yellow.

From here we made or way back to the hotel, on the way we passed a monkey family watching us watching them.

Derek had been feeling a bit off colour during the afternoon, so we spent the evening in our room, reading, catching up on the diary and enjoying a very good room service meal with wine.

In the morning we were in another convoy of 4x4s and our first stop was the Jaku hill temple, high on a wooded hill, the highest in Shimla at 8,038 feet. The temple is dedicated to the monkey god Hanuman. According to legend Hanuman rested here on his magical flight to fetch a herb that only grew in the Himalayas and was needed to save his love's life. The temple is now overrun by monkeys and there were many warnings about them and their thieving habits.

As we walked through the gardens, admiring the views, disaster struck. A seemingly docile monkey with her baby was sitting on a wall when she darted on to Fred's shoulder, snatched his glasses and ran off into the undergrowth. Wardens of the temple were summoned and an agile little man appeared with bag of peanuts who went in pursuit and eventually he returned with Fred's glasses. We set off again to visit Wildflower Hall, another architectural gem, formerly the country home of the Commander in Chief, Lord Kitchener, it is now a very up-market hotel, looking a bit like a French chateau, set in cedar and pine forests. The cream and black first and second storeys are set over grey stone. All the windows have small wrought iron balconies. We were delighted to be invited onto the terrace, where we enjoyed excellent coffee with home made biscuits under vast umbrellas to protet us from the hot sunshine. From the elegance and opulence of Wildflower Hall we drove to a tiny village, just one general store, and a bullock. In the fields there were huge coils of cable which, we were told, was to connect the village to the internet. India aims to have the whole population connected by 2012.

Our last call was at Woodville Palace, formerly the residence of generals in the British Army, temporarily seconded to India, now another up market Hotel., little changed since the 1930s. Behind the bar were photographs film stars of that period right up to Tom Cruise. Other memorabilia came from the Maharajahs. It was back then it was back to the Oberoi Hotel for a very good buffet dinner in the restaurant and then to bed as we were early off tomorrow on the toy train and the express back to Delhi.

We got up next day realising it was going to be a long day and long train journeys. Derek travelled in the stand-by car in some comfort with Sheila as both were regarded as a bit off colour still. The car stopped twice for facilities, cold drinks and comfortable shaded seats until it was time to move on. everyone else travelled on the toy train with one long stop at Barog station for passengers to use facilities and to get refreshments. Later the train had to stop because a fire on the hillside was blazing on the dry grass and spreading to the railway line and jumping across it. Eventually we got moving again, but the smoke was choking and we could feel the intense heat from the fires. Derek and Sheila may have had the comfort, but the rest of us had the excitement!

We were soon in Kalka, the Shatabdi Express was standing on Platform 2 and our carriage was open so we boarded and found our seats in Chair class across the aisle from three lively boys engaged in a wrestling match, which made us think we might have a tricky journey, but no. as the first refreshments arrived they were followed by a blonde no nonsense Australian lady, who came marching down the aisle to make sure the boys hands were clean. We chatted to her and she explained that there were two families travelling together; two mothers with five children.

The mother talking to us had three of the children, The fair one was her own son and one of the Indian boys and a lovely Indian girl was his sister. They had been adopted from an orphanage in Pune six years previously having spent six years in the iorphanage. The other family, and Indian boy and his sister further up the train also been adopted from the same orphanage at about the same time.

The mothers had decided that they must bring the children back to their roots to give them the opportunity to look for any extended family and to make sure that what they done in taking the children to Melbourne was really for the children and not for themselves. So, leaving their husbands behind, they had set off three weeks previously and "done" Delhi, Agra, Shimla, a safari, a bird reserve, elephant rides and Pune. The children decided they didn't like India as much as Australia, and certainly not the food, strangely none of them liked cricket!

Arriving in Delhi, we returned to the Claridges hotel and a splendid room this time. We had time for a light meal before off to bed in anticipating a very interesting day tomorrow as we boarded The Palace on Wheels for a different type of experience. When the day came we spent the morning relaxing and exchanging addresses with people we would like to keep in touch with, and then our final lunch at Claridges before the coach arrived to take us to a calm suburb of Delhi where the train slid in to the station and it was time for our welcome ceremony.

First we walked through a flower bedecked arch with a band playing to be greeted by sari-clad ladies who put the traditional red spot of welcome on our foreheads and a garland of flowers round our necks. Ladies were given a pretty red muslin scarf and men a large red turban with a long red tail. We were escorted to our carriage, jaisalmere and to our cabin number 4.It was more than adequate with two beds and a small bathroom wth toilet bathroom and shower, although storage and hanging space were limited.

Ours was one of four cabins in the carriage. We left at 6.30. We met for drinks before dinner and dined in the Maharini restaurant. Both bar and restaurants were train carriages, so you sit along the sides facing each other, so conversation is not easy. The two restaurants Maharajah and maharini were wonderfully decorated and set up for two sittings each evening and tables on each side of the central aisle were set for four. Most evenings we had second sitting, which was more relaxed as staff did not have to rush to setup for later diners.

Dinner was amazing; we had assumed from the menu that you chose what you wanted, either European or Indian, but not at all. The waiters just kept coming with different dishes so that you finished with a mixture of all sorts. We retired replete and slept well as the train continued through the night.

After a perfectly reasonable night's sleep we had a knock on the door at 6.15 followed by a very welcome tea and biscuits brought by San Josh, one of two attendants who travelled at the end of our carriage and were available 24 hours a day. He took our breakfast order for cereal or porridge, what variety of egg and how much toast. Breakfast was in a small breakfast room at the end of our carriage with three small, low settees set round a low table. we shared the room with our travelling companions, Lesley and Dan, William and Jennifer, and Ian our tour manager. We rarely found more than one other person at the same time.

We were about to arrive in Jaipur, so a few notes about it.Jaipur is about 60 miles south west of Delhi, and is capital of north west Rajahstan, founded in 1727 by Maharajah Jai Singh. It is encircled by 20 feet high City walls all painted pink because his astrologers said it was a significant colour for him. It is certainly one of India's most beautiful cities. By 8.00.a.m Beautifully decorated and dressed ceremonial elephants had arrived at the platform so we were ushered off the train to be given the traditional greeting of he floral garland and the red spot on the forehead before boarding our coach and going to the Royal Palace, "The Palace of the Winds" – one of the top sights of the trip, a five-storey building of lime and mortar painted pink and white. At ground level there are 13 columns, windows and balconies, but on each of the higher levels there are fewer and fewer rooms, so the outline is like that of a pyramid. The upper storeys are just one room deep and none of the walls are more than eight inches thick.

The lower windows have beautiful lattice work, but those at the top are tiny as they were for the women to peep through to see what was happening on the street below without themselves being seen. When we went down to the street there were lots of coaches and tourists, as well as hawkers including one there was a snake charmer with his cobras, one of which escaped, causing consternation among the tourists. Getting back to our coach required the combined efforts of a policeman and our guide to stop the traffic, showing little regard for pedestrians.

Next was the amber fort, some ten miles away. We could see it from a long way off as it sits on a hill, guarded by massive ramparts. Our entry through the ramparts was on elephants which involved mounting an elephant from a high platform to get onto the howdah. We, however were deemed either too small (Barbara) or too infirm (Derek) to manage that transfer, so we got the baby, which was a bit slow and we were overtaken by several bigger beasts especially when our baby stopped "for toilet" as our mahout put it and we arrived in the central courtyard to dismount. We walked through the first entrance into the second courtyard and into a second courtyard and to a lovely open pavilion with its double row of decorated marble and red sandstone pillars with a view across the fort. On te other side of the courtyard was a superb three storey ceremonial gateway decorated with floral motifs, mosaics and carved stonework, including latticed windows. The top storey windows orotrct the women in Purdah with decorated screens.. Walking through the arch we went into a cool courtyard with a colonnade of yellow and pink rows of columns.

The views down over the palace and its grounds were stunning. Then it was a walk round the formal geometrical gardens which were being re-constructed by three workers, two ladies and a man. The women, of course, were doing all the hard work, including carrying really heavy pans of soil and stones on their heads and still managing to look elegant. Across the garden was the mirror hall decorated with tiny mirrors embedded in finely carved pale sandstone which glittered and sparkled in the sun. At night it was it by hundreds of candles which must have been a magnificent sight. On the way out we passed the apartments for the maharajah's 12 wives. In the middle the apartments was a bathing pool so he was able, secretly to watch them as they bathed.

By now it was lunchtime, so we transferred to the Raj Palace hotel where a very good buffet was already laid out for us, after which a few of the party took the opportunity to have a quick swim in the hotel pool, and then we were off to the astronomy park, one of the most amazing sites we visited. Built between 1728 and 1734, and still used today it consists of 16 huge instruments resembling giant sculptures. The small sundial looks like a long flight of steps. It is constructed on Jaipur's latitude, 27 north and calculates local time to an accuracy of 20 seconds. An even larger sundial 75 feet high is used to forecast crop prospects for the year. Another set of instruments represented the signs of the zodiac and were used by astrologers to draw horoscopes. It was all mind boggling, especially when you realise that it had all been developed by one (very Clever) man 300 years ago.

The last visit was to the City Palace, a large complex that has been added to over the centuries by different rulers. We went into the first of the courtyards to a sandstone palace housing a superb display of textiles, dresses and polo equipment. Polo was played by a number of the moguls as well as later Indians and some of the British. From this area we could also the splendid seven storey Chandra Maha, still the residence of the present Maharajah. Were soon back on the coach and then to the train and our cabins to be welcomed by our attendants with cold towels, cups of tea and biscuits.

We woke the next morning at 5.45 a.m to draw back the curtains to see arid landscape whizzing by as we approached the remote outpost of Jaisalmer in the Thar Desert. In the scrub of thorn bushes were flocks of goats and scrawny sheep tended by a lonely goatherd.

After breakfast we were off to the Golden City, so called because as all its buildings are in golden yellow local sandstone. Jaisalmer was an important stop for the caravans plying the silk and opium route between Afghanistan and eastern Asia. There was the usual routine f red carpet, red spot of welcome, flower garland, and tis time a smartly uniformed guard at the station exit. The first stop was Gadisagar Lake south of the city walls, It was a rain water reservoir built in 1367, and once the only source of drinking water for the city. The water was low as the monsoons had failed for a number of years, but it was still a pretty place, especially with the reflections of temples surrounding it..The gateway leading to the lake has a charming story about. The gateway was built by a royal courtesan, Telia,but the fact that she had had it built it so enraged the Queen at the time that she ordered that it be demolished, but Telia was clever and immediately had a statue of Krishna put on the top. This ensured it would not be destroyed, but also meant that the Queen and other rulers had to bow to enter.

We walked back to the coach which transferred us to the coach park where a number of Tuk Tuks were waiting to whisk us up to the fort, the only lived-in fort in India, with an estimated 3,500 Iiving in, or crammed into, it. There was a great atmosphere but it gid seem very crowd narrow streets to reach ited, especially with all the sacred cows and their cowpats. We were to visit the Jain temple which was some way inside the fort and we had to weave our way through narrow streets to reach it. The Jains respect all life, so we had to remove anything with leather.as well as shoes we removed belts, bags and watches with leather straps, all kept safe in one of the shops. They are also strict vegans ad wear masks so as to avoid breathing in any living creature.

Having retrieved our belongings, we walked through the bazaar with lots of people, but not oppressive. The streets were full of delicious fruits and vegetables brought in from the country and laid on tables. There was an amusing incident as we passed a side street where a game of cricket was taking place among some boys. Two members of our group decided to join in and show off their prowess at batting and bowling. They were thrashed!

We had really liked Jaisalmere; it was one of our favourite places, but we had to return to our train, as we were going out to dinner.

Dinner tonight was to include a cultural display at the Gorbandh Palace hotel. The cultural show came first in a pleasant covered courtyard where we were entertained by three ladies in traditional costume, singing and dancing. They invited anyone to join them. The only volunteer was Jennifer, a retired ballerina who was able to follow their movements precisely. Dinner was a buffet, with a menu similar to those in other venues.

And so we go to Jodhpur. Having been to the pink city of Jaipur and the golden city of Jaiselmer, we are now headed for the blue city of Jodhpur, beautifully set out below us as we reached the site of the original crematorium and the present memorial to Jaswant Singh II and his relatives. From the coach we walked past the place where once mourners washed before entering the crematorium. Nowadays bathrooms have replaced it. The memorial or Cenotaph is set high and is made of fine white marble with fantastic carvings, towers, balconies and domes, all framed with vivid yellow acacias.

Below the main memorial were others to his wives and lower still, his uncles..Their memorials were decorated with at least one horseshoe, as they were all keen polo players. Later we passed a large area strung with washing lines on which were bright sheets of material drying after being dyed.

To get to the fort our coach had to negotiate a sharp right turn and unfortunately we met a press car coming the other way. There was only room for one vehicle at a time so there was a stand off between the drivers, but eventually our driver gave way because he had foreign visitors onboard ad we were on our way. looking up we could see the ramparts which completely surround the city; the fort high on the hill,and across, through the haze, the palace, now a hotel, and where we would have our lunch.

The fort was sitting on a sheer rock face, so we used the lift and emerged onto the ramparts, the walls of which were hewn from the rock itself. From here we went into the Maharini's courtyard which was surrounded by delicate pale sandstone buildings with more of the fantastic carvings we had seen in other forts. there was a gruesome relic of earlier times in the footprints of 15 previous maharinis who had performed suttee on the funeral pyres of their dead husbands.(suttee is an ancient Hindu practice whereby a woman jumped onto the pyre of their dead Husbands in order to join him in Paradise). We then went into a small museum, which was very interesting.

Here were palanquins, a covered cabin, usually carried by four or six bearers on ceremonial occasions. The highlights of this fort were rooms built between 1500 and 1700 of extreme opulence; one of them used for royal celebrations and entertainment. The walls were in rich teak gilded and painted in bright colours, with beautiful stained glass in the windows. the bedroom was just as grand with a tiled floor, carved wooden ceiling, arched and decorated walls. The most spectacular was the audience room where visiting dignitaries would be received. A red carpet on the floor echoed the red in big stained glass windows. Around the edges of the room were cushions on which visitors sat. Opposite the windows was a wall with dozens of niches for candles to be placed in the evening to make an awe-inspiring sight. There were three doorways; during a reception for an ambassador, these were hidden by curtains so that three favourite wives could secrete themselves there, listen to the conversation ad ten give advice to the maharajah.

We gradually made our way down, calling en route at some very clean toilets, though toilet paper was rationed! We were heading for lunch at the Palace hotel, where we got the full red carpet and fancy canopy treatment. It was a huge palace with 300 rooms in the palace as a whole, with one wing remained the current residence of the maharajah. After a splendid lunch we left to rejoin Palace on Wheels. We left Jodhpur at 3.30 p.m. towards the tiger reserve tomorrow.

The alarm went at 4.45 a.m for yet another early start. We had coffee and toast and set off at 5.30 for the jeeps that were to take us into the Rathnambore National Park, a 15 minute drive away. We were in the front jeep with some jolly Australians and Ian and were off along rough dirt tracks, driver river beds and negotiating over hanging branches and large boulders, pausing often to listen for bird alarm calls (which might indicate the presence of big cats, and to look at other wild life of the park: lots of birds including peahens, as well as the peacock displaying his magnificent tail, big kingfishers, noisy rose ring parakeets, colourful tree pies, robins, bee eaters, serpent eagles, honey buzzards, herons and lapwings, not a bit like ours at home. here were all sorts of deer, pygmy crocodiles and families of mongoose; but where are the tigers ? Suddenly there was some excitement ahead, and there right in front of us was a fantastic female tiger. She crossed slowly in front of us, heading for the river, where she stopped for a drink. It was a heart-stopping moment to see this superb creature and her reflection in the water until she disappeared into the long grass, where her camouflage was so perfect that we momentarily lost her, but she re-emerged and we watched her until she lay down. What an experience!

Back at the train for lunch, after we had a most interesting journey through a different part of rural India passing by our window. We saw dwellings of the poorest, just shacks along the road or the railway. Running water was rarely available, so they relied on one village pump where we saw women queuing for their turn and using the wait for a gossip.

We left the train for the hilltop fort of Chittorgargh at 4.p.m.. To get into the fort we had to negotiate the features of the building set to deter invaders, first were seven narrow gates. Seven was important because the ancients believed it was a magic number, as in seven days in a week, colours of the rainbow and seven white horses to pull the sun chariot.. For negotiating our entrance we were in the hands of the coach driver. The first easy gate faced east, the second was narrow, meaning only centimetres between the coach and the thick rock walls. The third had vicious spikes sticking out from the walls to deter elephants, the fourth had Ganesh on top to put off any enemies, to get to the fifth and sixth required dealing with much reversing and shunting round of U bends. Finally we made it through all the obstacles and arrived at the last gate, a beautifully carved sandstone entrance to what is the home of 5,000 people, who can boast of 56 generations of Maharajahs. The nearby temple was built over an original sun temple. An old priest sat giving sugar to the faithful, although we never found out why.

The nine-storey Victory Tower dominates this area at 1158 feet high in rich red sandstone carved with gods and goddesses. It is extraordinary in that it has a broad base and elaborate first storey, the next four storeys taper upwards, gradually getting smaller, but then the top storeys are wider, heavier and balconied very striking

After tea, cold drinks and biscuits to sustain us. and the use of facilities, we made our way to the setting for Son et Lumiere, which was delightful. Nightfall came quickly so the sky was like black velvet spangled with stars. It was warm after the heat of the day, and peacefully quiet. The show was magnificent with the lighting of different parts of the building. The sound, the story and the narration were brilliant. Only the music proved a bit of a challenge.

Last night, during dinner, the train moved forward 5 km s e could have a quiet night. set off again early morning to reach the fairy tale city of Udaipur, popular with tourists because of the splendour of its buildings and the opulence of it's interiors. it has a proud heritage of remaining Hindu during the Moghul period, resisting Muslim influence fr at least fifty years longer than other Indian states. We drove through the white town, admiring the lake and it's surrounding hills. We went on to the Garden of fountains, entering through a great red and white entrance. Inside were borders full of canna flowers and gladioli. Our guide welcomed us to the garden and asked us to clap loudly to acknowledge the welcome. We did as instructed and were suddenly surrounded on both sides by high fountauins; it was a surprise, but a nice one.

It was then on to the next garden, The Lotus Blossom, which was a mass of otus flowers, some in bloom, some in bud. Once again we were asked to clap and the fountains rose from the pool in the centre.

The city palace was a huge place part residence of the maharajah, part museum and part hotel. There was some exquisite workmanship and is a complex of several palaces built by 22 maharajahs between the 16th and 20th centuries. From a number of the rooms there were lovely views of Lake Pichola. Inside we admired delicate fretwork, elegant columns, marble relief work and superb balconies jutting out from the walls of the main building, but it was very hot and we were all a little palace weary by this time, so we were glad to get into the hotel area, where it was cool with opulent toilets and an excellent buffet lunch in the Durbar hall.

After lunch we walked down to the lake where we had a gentle boat ride round the lake and were able to see the haveli, palaces and bridges from a different perspective as well as women doing the washing from the steps down to the lake, and the men and boys swimming happily. The birds were another pleasure. We saw kingfishers, swallows, grebes, cormorants, and storks,not a bad list for one afternoon. Getting off the boat we realised how hot it still was, so it was back to the train. The colds cloths and the cups of tea served to us in the cabin were very welcome.

The next morning was quite marvellous and strangely unexpected. It was a short ride to the bird sanctuary where we got into pedal rickshaws. The atmosphere in the reserve was utterly tranquil and tranquillity is scarce in India. It was a cool, balmy morning with only bird calls and clean with no litter. The birding was excellent, especially round the little lake, where all manner of birds and deer gathered to feed and drink. The early start had been worth it!

The train left for Agra soon after 9.a.m. We arrived three hours Later with our bags packed, cabin cleared and bills paid. No more Palace on Wheels! We watched as our bags were loaded into the van. Before lunch our schedule took us to the Agra fort, built 1565-1573, is a beautiful building, described in guide books as "A serenade in Sandstone". Lunch was at the Mughal Sheraton, the hotel where we would be staying the night. in rom 367. It had been a very early start on a very hot day,so resting in this lovely room was very tempting but we were going to the Taj. he coach took us to the outskirts, but then we were transferred to electric vehicles for the rest of the way to limit the pollution. Because it is so well known and photographed, nothing quite prepares you for your first sight of the Taj Mahal, one of the seven wonders of the world, a pristine monument to undying love built by the emperor Shah Jahan in memory of his beloved queen, Mumtaz Mahal. Some of you may remember a famous photograph on Princess Diana sitting alone on a bench in front of the Taj Mahal during her early marital troubles. We have a photograph of both of us on the same bench, glad to say we do not have marital troubles.

After a goodnights sleep and a leisurely breakfast we climbed on to the coach to return to Delhi through endless traffic jams until we eventually arrived back at The Claridges again to a lovely room at the side of the pool, ready for the farewell dinner in the hotel before our last sleep in India

Chapter 5

South Africa: Political prisoners,
frightened monkeys and dinner in a cave

Although this chapter is in Part Two for countries we visited mainly by train, it scarcely qualifies as our booking was for a tour arranged by Great Rail journeys, A telephone call shortly before we departed advised us with great regret that there were serious floods along parts of the route that the train would not be able o cope with, so there three choices: 1. Take a full refund and cancel the trip. 2. Transfer the booking to next year. 3. Continue although many stretches would be by coach.

Option 3 could only proceed if there were at least 15 takers. We decided we would take Option 3 and shortly afterwards we assembled somewhere in Cape Town arrivals as part of a group of 14 together with Tour Manager Ian Stanley(who had shepherded us round India the year before), so we loaded our bags onto a coach to take us to The Cullinan Hotel, where we were to lodge for the first part of our trip. After settling into our rooms, we gathered in the garden for our first briefing from Ian. As we had arrived in Cape Town quite early, we had the rest of the morning to potter about in the immediate locality and have lunch, before gathering in the hotel foyer at 2 p.m.

for our first tour to Robben Island, where Nelson Mandela had been imprisoned before his famous "Long walk to freedom". We pottered quite happily as far as Green market square where we had lunch in the company's gardens, without knowing what the company was.

At 2.p.m. we were all assembled and taken to a quayside to board the ferry for Robben Island, the previous leper colony that had been turned into a prison for political prisoners, that is political activists who had campaigned for an end to white only rule and denial of voting rights to blacks. Britain and Holland had competed with each other for colonising South Africa and its vast mineral resources. This was partly resolved by the Boer wars at the end of the 19th century, whereby Britain colonised the bulk of the country and the boers (who called themselves Voortrekkers) took over Transvaal and the Orange Free State, establishing their language of Afrikaans and their Dutch Reformed Church. By the time of our visit the situation was quite different. Mandela had been released, universal suffrage for all adults had been established.

It was a short ferry crossing and we were allocated a guide who was an ex freedom fighter and gun runner, who had been imprisoned for six and a half years in a different women' prison. She showed us round the prison block, which was a quadrangle of austere single rooms, each with a window that opened. She showed us into what had been Mandela's room, with a coir mat, a single bed, a desk and chair. Outside we visited a limestone quarry where the prisoners worked and Mandela met with some of his supporters to plan how they would deal with their future government, which they regarded as inevitable.

As a contrast we saw the old leper graveyard, a smart modern school for children who live on the island and a small number of the Cape penguin colony on the island.

Then it was back on the ferry to the mainland, a short walk to the Cullinan and up to room 1401 to get ready for the evening; a little bit special as t was our ruby (40th) wedding anniversary and we were going out to dinner, with Barbara sporting a brand new ruby ring, we walked down to the waterfront and enjoyed an excellent with the essential bottle of champagne. Then back again to room1401 to bed and anticipating the Cape of Good Hope tomorrow.

Waking up the next morning we looked out of our window across to the top of Table mountain and saw that it was shrouded in mist, which was not encouraging for our expedition, but at breakfast Ian told us that the coach would collect us at 2.p.m, giving the heavy mist to dissipate. Some notes on The Cape: it marks the southern tip of Africa, the point where the European traveller stops travelling south and turns east, first discovered in 1488 by the Portuguese navigator Bartholomew Diaz, so opening up sea routes to India and beyond to European adventurers, colonisers and traders

As soon as 12 years later a Portuguese diplomat on his way to India on a mission, almost by accident, discovered the land we now know as Brazil, the largest country in South America.

The weather has not improved by lunch time, but we set off in the coach anyway and came to a smallish building, supposedly marking the spot, although recent geographical analysis shows it to be 19 miles wrong. There are two cafes, toilets and a shop. It is raining quite hard, so we stay indoors, but suddenly there is a commotion as dozens of monkeys, frightened by driving winds in gusts whipping up the rain, and the monkeys go beserk.

Despite the wild weather yesterday, we drew back the curtains today to find the sun shining, so we decided to go up Table Mountain, the 1,080 metres flat-topped mountain across the bay from Cape Town, having first established that there was a cable car ! We took the cable car and arrived at the top to find lovely views and Dassies or rock hyrax, which are badger -like small animals that are to be found mainly on Table Mountain where they are common. Another discovery was fynbos, a scrub-like vegetation all over the mountain. The name is Afrikaans for fine bush, a pretty neat definition.

Descending to Cape Town once more we pass by Cape Town Cathedral, where Archbishop Desmond Tutu is conducting a wedding. Later we pass back behind the building where Derek sees him in the garden, wearing a T shirt, very different from his episcopal robes, so he says in surprise, "Oh, good afternoon," which elicited the response "Hi!" – decidedly not episcopal.

The next day we set off for our re-organised coach tour along the coast from Cape Town to Mossell Bay and back. Most of the floods had begun to subside. Our first call is at the Anura vineyard, where we watch grapes being pressed by the traditional method of a young man treading grapes barefoot in a large cask with the juice being drained off for processing. Although it is only 9.30 we then have a wine tasting of several wines, being grateful that we are not driving, but one or two heads nod as we are driven on to the Spier hotel in Stellenbosch for lunch where the restaurant had been under 4feet of floodwater 12 hours earlier. From there we move on to a cheetah rescue and rehabilitation centre, before finishing at an ostrich farm where one female was under a shelter sitting on seven eggs. Males could be raced or ridden apparently without coming to harm as long as the riders were not too heavy, as judged by its minder. Just one of our fellow travellers (Les.) had a go, and was quite shaken up afterwards. Finally the coach took us to the Outeniqua pass for our hotel for the night. From our room we could see the pass in one direction and the lagoon, with many sailing ships in the other. After a busy day we had dinner in the hotel and then an early night.

Refreshed and well breakfasted we set of for our tour of Knysna, a wonderful bay with pounding waves and scope for all manner of beach and other holiday activities, making it a popular destination for vacations. After lunch we return to the hotel and prepare for our next adventure, dinner in a cave!

We gradually assembled around 7-ish at the "Wilderness" station for the train that will take us to the cave. It turns out to be a set of converted cable cars that take us half a mile along the side of a cliff to a large cave where a dinner table is set with a white cloth stretching into the cave and laid with all the necessary cutlery and glassware and menus, all lit by candles. One converted cable car had preceded us bringing in a team of waiters to serve us. We all ate and drank very well, although not to excess of course, until it was time to return on the train and then the coach to the hotel, to begin thinking of the elephants tomorrow

In the morning the coach took us to an elephant park, where elephants of all ages were to be found, including a baby that Barbara took a shine to and Elfie fed some of the older ones. In India we had seen many working elephants, mostly moving timber, but those we saw in Knysna (The only African elephants we saw) did not seem to be put to work at all. From the Elephants we were driven down to the water front for lunch at a very up-market restaurant on the beach.

Then it was back to the hotel to check out and then join a train with the odd name of, Outenia - tchoo - tjoe,to take us to Mossel Bay for our last night in Mossel Bay Hotel before turning back towards Cape town. Almost as soon as the train left Knysna it reached a 2 kilometer viaduct curving round the bay. When we checked in we were allocated a splendid room with windows overlooking a natural swimming area, often used by some of our more sturdy fellow travellers.

It was only over night in Mossel Bay and then it was back in the bus for the return to Cape Town, although we had stop on the way to see the Steam Train Graveyard, which was popular with a very few people! We later had a small tour of the voortrekker area of Cape Town, where we saw Auld Huse., the oldest house in Swellendam, dated 1802, and The Dutch Reformed Church with seating for 1,000 people. We saw the voortrekker monument, surrounded by granite ox wagons representing how the settlers travelled.

Next day was a distinct change as we were driven to a safari lodge, the Kwa maritane for a few days, where we had a suite on the first floor with a balcony overlooking the gardens and the rest of the reserve as far as a water hole for animals to drink. We had two safari drives when we saw antelopes,wild dogs, rhinos and zebras. Throughout our short stay we had all our meals at the outdoor restaurant buffet.

At the end of our short stay, we were driven back to Cape town with a stop at Lesedi cultural village, where we were welcomed by mothers, children, old and young, all arrayed in traditional tribal costumes. They sang and danced for our entertainment before serving us with a very acceptable buffet lunch. We then walked round the village to see traditional crafts being demonstrated. Ladies in our party were particularly interested in ladies doing intricate bead craft. Then we were off to Cape Town for The last time before we board the famous Blue Train to take us overnight to Pretoria

Leaving Cape Town this time was unusual as we had a little time to enjoy this lovely city after returning from the cultural village, so we chose to spend part of it on the Victoria and Alfred waterfront which we had found to be very good for watching the world go by while eating ice cream and drinking a cup of tea. This time it was embellished when a very clever mime artist came up behind Derek and slightly to one side, following him step by step for some way to the great amusement of Barbara and various passers-by.

Having already mentioned that we were enjoying our ruby

wedding anniversary, it is now necessary to mention that another couple, Harry and Enid, were also enjoying a significant wedding anniversary, their twenty fifth. That evening we had just gone to bed, when we were aware of Ian rushing along the corridor carrying a bottle of wine in an ice bucket. He paused briefly at our door, then rushed further along. Shortly afterwards he knocked on our door and presented us with a bottle of Champagne in an ice bucket, with a note from Great British Rail Journeys. It later transpired that Harry and Enid had received a similar gift. We slept very well.

We described our dinner in a cave as an adventure. Our journey from Cape town to Pretoria was a series of surprises. We assembled for the last time in the foyer of The Cullinan, soon to have a group photograph taken b efore before boarding our transport (an ex london double decker bus) to the Blue Train departure lounge, where we waited in comfort, rather like the first class lounge in an airport, with drinks and light snacks, as a waiter came and checked each person off his list and distributed keys for suites and table numbers in the restaurant. Then stewards arrived to escort us to our suites, advising that lunch in the restaurant would be at 12.30. By 12.15 we were on our way on the 1,600 km journey to Pretoria and taking it easy in our suite before moving through to the restaurant for a very pleasant lunch and placing our orders for dinner at first sitting at 7.00 or second at 8.00

After lunch we sat and enjoyed the passing scene outside our window over a cup of tea until the train gradually slowed for the only scheduled stop before Pretoria: Matjies fontein, a solitary relic of the Boer War, where it had been a marshalling station and supply centre for the British Army Since then it seems to have been in steady decline with a small population totally dependent on passengers from the Blue train. We were invited to step off the train, which would wait for an hour. During that time a fellow who was a general handyman and dogsbody to the town led passengers like a pied piper around the main points of interest, calling out at each, "It's show time."

When our time was up it was back on the train and on non-stop to Pretoria, where Ian took us to a modest hotel for the night with instructions not to go outside at all because it would be dangerous! Eventually food of the pizza and chips variety was brought in and Derek made a short speech of thanks to Ian, who was presented with a small teddy bear called Blue, after the train. Next morning we were bussed to Johannisberg airport to catch our various flights home. after a memorable and most enjoyable tour

Part Three

Mainly by ocean or river cruising.

Chapter 6

Bali: A short cruise, where
we meet a dangerous lizard

Bali is a volcanic island off the east coast of Java in Indonesia, and is one of the great tourist resorts of the world. We travelled there from Kuala Lumpur (KL)and boarded a small ship, "Oceanic Odyssey" for a week's sailing, calling at various islands on the way. We were late arriving because of a belated departure of the flight from a new airport at KL, which was handling passengers for the first time with almost inevitable muddle and uncertainties. We had flown in to the old airport the previous evening. Much of this chapter covers the time we spent on the other islands.

It was a small ship with some 20 to 25 passengers. We were comfortably accommodated and very well fed. The first island we called in at for a few hours was Sulawesi, where we were entertained to a race between bullock carts pulled by oxen across a flooded rice field. were shown items of furniture and curtains that were kept from the time of Dutch occupation. The whole of Indonesia was Dutch until 1940 when they were displaced by the Japanese, who were displaced by allied forces in 1945, when they were liberated by British troops. Then European colonies in the east were gradually replaced by nationalist governments, typically peacefully and occasionally reluctantly. In the mid 1980s derek spent some time on working visits to Malaysia which had gained its independence from Britain in 1957, although Singapore, at the foot of the Malay peninsula, having a mainly Chinese population, remained a British Crown colony, eventually becoming an independent republic. In Malaysia he met a number of people using the phrase "The good old days" about British rule.

Continuing our sailing, we stopped at Yogyakarta from where we had an excellent view of the volcano mount agung, which had only wisps of smoke lazily drifting from the summit. In 1963 it had erupted, killing thousands of people and causing economic havoc. Jogyakarta itself has an eighteenth century royal complex or Kraton, which is still in use as Yogyakarta is the only province of Indonesia ruled by a monarchy. Around the Kraton were numerous stalls and shops to tempt tourists and several Gamalan orchestras, which are strange to the western ear including gongs and stringed instruments.

The following day we went, with two American couples, for a morning excursion to see two temples, Perambanan (Hindu) and Borobudor (Buddhist). both were fascinating, but most of us preferred the second, which was built in 842 with an inscription saying that Borobudur was built "For the accumulation of virtue in the ten stages of the Bodhisattvas". It had fallen into disuse for centuries until eventually being rediscovered by Sir Stamford Raffles, who was \British Governor General at the time. It is a massive and impressive building.

We had booked the tour the previous day and only met the other two couples when we found we were all sharing a minibus; they were not from our ship. It was a very hot day and on the way back in the minibus the two other men were at the front, the two other women in the middle and we were at the back. Soon general conversation lapsed and the two of us started talking quietly about our programme for the next day. By the time we reached the drop-off point for the others, the two women had to be roused, and they said that our English accents and speech were so smooth that it lulled them to sleep. We then had to decide whether we were flattered or affronted. One of the husbands went into their hotel and brought us out two bottles of Coca-Cola.

The next day disaster struck. It was hotter than ever as we sailed along to our next island, Komodo, but long before we got there the engine broke down. The ship came to a halt and the air conditioning stopped.. We could still eat, drink and sunbathe but the cabins were soon stiflingly hot and life generally became complicated as the engineers slaved away below decks to solve the problem and we sought out whatever shade was to be found on deck and the chef offered what food he could manage. when dusk fell it brought little relief as the temperature remained very high. we all gradually decided to sleep on deck, having collected as much of our bed clothes as we could carry. Sleep was intermittent but by morning there was a slightly cool breeze.

After breakfast and a brief return to the cabin, there came the welcome news from the captain that the problem was fixed and we should soon be on the way to our next island, Komodo.

Readers with long memories may recall a television programme by a young David Attenborough called "In search of a dragon". The dragon in question is the world's largest Monitor lizard, which is only to be found in small numbers in Komodo island and three smaller islands in this area, Flores, Rinca. and Gil Motang. A popular rumour among tourist operators is that the animal's saliva is lethal to humans and that a visiting Swedish naturalist ventured on to the island alone and was never seen again, although his spectacles were found in undergrowth on the far side of the island. Along with everyone else on the ship, we were going ashore.

We were put into two groups, each accompanied by a crew member carrying a first aid kit! Any incipient apprehension was alleviated our local guide, who was carrying just a stout forked stick. As we walked along behind our guide we passed the one village on the island, raised on stilts. As we moved on he pointed out Monitors: males that typically reached 10 to 20 feet in length and females up to 6 feet. They are carnivores with a diet of pigs, deer and occasionally chicken, but they are also cannibals and a small part of their diet is newly born baby monitors. Hastily moving on we were shown a fire pit for cooking meat and declined the guide's offer of a demonstration chicken for 5 dollars. We left with no liking for monitors, their diet, nor the reassurance that they did attack humans, but only rarely! Their proper scientific name, apparently, is kudoensis

Moving on from Komodo we had a brief stop at the island of Lombok and then back to Bali, where we disembarked and we moved into a hotel for two nights during which we saw Balinese dancing, music and mask-making. The masks are a local speciality. They are purely decorative We have two in our entrance hall and so far they have not alarmed any visitors.

Life under canvas in France with our young family

Arriving at Taman Negara National Park, Malaysia

Ceremonial dancers at Bankok Royal Place, Thailand

Keeping the traffic moving in Shimla,
capital of Himachel Pradesh, India

The author about to board The
Palace on Wheels train, Rajasthan, India

The Taj Mahal, India, tomb of the favourite
wife of the 7th-century Mughal emperor Shah Jahan

Limestone quarry on Robben Island, South Africa,
where the imprisoned Nelson Mandela planned his future

Converted cable car in which we were
taken to dinner in a cave in Knysna, South Africa

*Young seller of matroyoschas (Russian dolls)
outside Kostroma, Russia*

Catherine The Great's Winter Palace, St Petersburg, Russia

Tramway into the rain forest in Costa Rica

Chicken Itza Pyramid World Heritage Site, Mexico

Fruit seller outside the dock in Maldive

Brits sunning themselves on the deck of the cruise ship Minerva

Gulfoss (Golden Falls) waterfall, South Iceland

Chapter 7
Adriatic Odyssey: A cruise aboard Minerva 2014

Our day started at the ridiculously early time of 5am but we were soon off driving to Manchester Airport. We had to find Meet and Greet in Terminal 3, one we had not used before. However, once there it was very straight forward. We left the car and checking in was easy and efficient and the lounge was comfortable. As Derek needed a wheel chair we had assistance and we were taken right to the gate by a very pleasant assistance man, so avoiding the queue.

At Heathrow we had to wait on the plane because of "congestion", so we were directed to an international area.. It took some time for the congestion to clear The lounge was really very good; drinks and breakfast; we were there so long we had lunch as well. We had a delay of three hours due to debris on the runway and there were no flights in or out until it was cleared.

When the time for boarding was finally called, we were deposited in the fast lane where we waited until boarding. Good seats and good meals. a veggie meal was found for Barbara even though it wasn't on the system, good champagne and a good flight.

Due to the delay we arrived in Rome very late but after an efficient coach transfer to Minerva, two and a half hours after we had been expected. They had kept the Veranda dining room open and served a full meal. After supper, our cases had arrived in the cabin so we unpacked to find the essentials before collapsing into bed. The time was 12.15 local time, we had been up 18 hours!

The next day we were in Piraeus, the port for Athens, where some of our fellow passengers were off early on a trip to Corinth. After the very long day yesterday we felt it was better to just chill and remind ourselves of Minerva. After breakfast we walked into the terminal and bought a bottle of water, still muttering about not having free water provided. Lunch time really set the cruise off to a great start. We had a Greek buffet outside on Veranda. It was delicious, and for some there was the usual choice inside.

We sailed at 1pm for the Corinth canal. As it was the first sailing we had, of course, to do boat drill with the usual information from the captain and the amusing sights of passengers putting on, with varying degrees of success, their life jackets. At 3pm we went to listen to "The cruise in perspective". It was interesting to see the different personalities of our lecturers.

At 5pm we began the transit of the canal; the day was a bit grey but the Canal wove its magic and nearly all the passengers were out on deck to watch the bridges, the high cliffs and the amazing navigation of the pilots taking the ship through the Canal with inches to spare on each side. Barbara was one of the people right at the front of ship and there were, of course, lots of photographers there. One of them, a very tall American, chose to use her head as his tripod!

The canal is 6 km long, 23 m wide at its widest, and 8 m deep. At one point the cliffs rise nearly 92m above the ship. During the passage of the Canal we were "treated" to a glass of ouzo. We had dinner with Pam and Janet, a very nice couple from Norfolk. Barbara thought they might never dine with us again after they decided one of Derek's tales was "too much information", though they did, several times.

The next day was a typical Minerva day at sea. There were lectures by Andrew Burnett, Deputy director of the British Museum, Ian Beckett, Professor of military history at the University of Kent, Andrew Hopkins, professor at the University of L;Aquila, and the first craft workshop with Karin Bucannan. We had a balcony for our cabin, so we enjoyed the sunshine as we sailed through the Greek islands.

In the evening it was the captain's welcome party with sparkling wine and a canapés. The following meal was very good, the service excellent and the company pleasant with Keith and Heather with whom we were to have a lot more pleasant contact.

Next day we had moved on to Kotor in Croatia. it was delightful to visit Kotor again and to remember the sail up the fjord. We chose to go on the Montenegro panorama excursion and it was a lovely trip, though some of the roads were hair raising! We had an interesting guide who told us how Montenegro had adopted the German euro since 2002 because of the massive inflation of the Dinar so the only way for the people to survive was to give up its own currency.

Another interesting bit of information was that until recently the practise of arranged marriage was quite common. The family believed the daughters would be safe from the Turkish soldiers and their "Bloody revenge" if they were married. Even so, fathers kept a close watch on the marriage and if there was any violence or suffering in the home the father could legitimately kill the husband!

We were soon distracted by the views on the "Adrenalin" road. It had at least 27 hairpin bends so looking down certainly was scary. Even looking across the valley at the Donkey path was stomach churning. For centuries the tiny narrow path was the Sunday trading route between Njegusi, the village we were heading for, and Kotor.

The village was tiny and looked quite poor but the local crafts were soon on display as soon as the coach parked. There were lace and embroidered cloths, coats, knitted jumpers and hats. No doubt done with love during the long winter days but not perhaps to our tastes. There were also food stalls with hams and cheeses. We went to the small café where we were served with the local delicacies, ham and cheese, on huge slabs of local bread. They were interesting and delicious. They were washed down by local beer, wine or soft drinks..

The members of the group boarded the coach in a good mood and we were on the way to Cetinje, the former capital, to see the King's Palace, a museum since 1926. After parking the coach we walked a short way to a modern town square, surrounded by a variety of buildings. We approached a modest looking building, which was the palace Its modesty resulted from the 500 years war with the Turks when it escaped attack because of its appearance, like that of a typical house of the region and not a Royal residence.

Inside there was a collection of portraits of the Royal family, furniture and silver much of which was original dating from the 1700s to 1921. The wallpaper and the floors were copies of the originals which were damaged in the world wars.

After wandering through the not very impressive palace, we went through an even less impressive gift shop and down a very steep set of steps to the garden. which was fairly unloved. It had once been a flower garden with roses but few remained. Beyond was a row of pines that led to a cedar grove.

Across the road was a tiny white chapel which housed the coffins of the last king and queen of Montenegro. The king was known as "The King of Hearts" because of his lack of opulence and show, and his care for his people. He had been brought up in a modest house in a village famous for its hams and had played with and gone to school with the village children and thus got to appreciate the needs of his subjects. The king had his ashes scattered, as was the tradition, on the second highest peak in the country in order to leave the highest peak "for a better man". No-one has proved better and now a simple mausoleum stands on that second peak.

We walked through the trees and back to the car park. There was the usual pause for the toilet. This proved rather a challenge for 'Beryl'. At the very moment she arrived there was no attendant so, reasonably, she walked into the 'facility' and immediately an attendant emerged demanding payment, she ignored this and the demand became rather more insistent. A coin was produced but it wasn't a euro, so no good. Husband then got involved giving a rea) euro "for two of them". That wouldn't do either. It had to be *50 cents* per person or no visit. At this point husband found a 50cent, gave it to bloke collecting the money who was still trying, unsuccessfully, to stop Beryl going into the toilet and disappeared. The episode had involved not only Beryl and husband but a significant number of Swans trying to be helpful and locals enjoying the show

The onward drive took us towards Budva. We passed rows and rows of second hand cars, dozens of them. This was where you came if you wished to buy a car, though getting a licence to drive was certainly demanding. You started at 18 with 18 months of practical tuition that included car mechanics, first aid and driving theory. In the test a driving instructor was present as well as two policemen. If you passed that you held it for 10 years but then had to have another test as well as a medical and this happened every 10 years.

Budva didn't impress us. It seemed very tacky and touristy with lots of hotels, apartments, casinos and venues for 'night parties'.

Back on board, lunch was a delicious oriental buffet on the veranda, where the concept of a "little" spice and chilli had different interpretations between chef and consumer. After lunch we strolled into Kotor and were a bit disappointed that the green market we had seen from the coach had packed away all its greens. We walked in through the grand entrance which bears the memorial arms and the quote *"What belongs to others we don't want, what is ours we will never surrender."* Apt in view of its troubled history.

Even with a map of the town we couldn't make out where we were and which church/cathedral was which, so we just enjoyed Kotor, its iconic clock tower, its small churches as well as the bigger cathedral of St. Typhon, the tiny streets with washing hanging from the upper windows and the little belfry on the roof of an insignificant church. As ever we marvelled at the exquisite iconostases in the cathedral, the Serbian Orthodox Church and the very tiny chapel that had room for only half a dozen people at once. We had a drink sitting just outside the walls before walking back and chilling out.

Minerva left Kotor at 5pm and had a delightful sail along the Bay of Kotor, or the Boka, towards the sea. We passed the two picturesque islands opposite the little town of Perast. The first island is the island of St. George which is also known as "The Island of the Dead". because it has a very old cemetery which houses hundreds or even thousands of sailors, clergy and noblemen of the area.

Under the tall forbidding cypresses lies the "city" of the dead that apparently has a dining room and cell-like bedrooms alongside many tombstones with the coats of arms of the buried. It is also known as "the hidden" as it is supposed to hide vast treasures of art. No tourists are allowed to visit and it is mainly lived in in July and August by Roman Catholic clergy on retreat. They now have electricity, running water and five bathrooms as well as the dining room. The island is also home to a Benedictine monastery.

The second island is that of "Our Lady of the Reef", is the only artificial island in the Adriatic. Legend has it that two fishermen on July 22nd 1452 found an icon of the Madonna and Child on a rock and one of them was immediately cured of an illness. In gratitude he threw more rocks on the site of the original one; since then all fishermen returning safely from their trip throw a rock there. As well as the rocks the people of Perast sank all the pirate ships they'd captured so that now there is a sizeable island with a Roman Catholic Church. The tradition of the rocks still persists and every July 22nd the local people sail across to add more rocks.

This evening's meal was awkward as we were put on a table for six, which is usually OK but this night we were joined by four others; Emma who was from near Vancouver, having left her husband (an A&E consultant) and four children at home; her mother, Bridget, with whom she was travelling, a Conservative councillor and a couple who somehow had a connection with Bridget's sister, though they had never met up previously. All four then proceeded to totally ignore us. We suddenly became invisible, which was most uncomfortable so we escaped as soon as possible

The evening was rescued by the entertainment provided by a duo: a pianist who provided the appropriate accompaniment to pieces by the actor Carole Boyd, Linda Snell of Archer fame. Several of the pieces she did were in the voice and character of Linda Snell, which was most amusing.

Our next port of call was Dubrovnik in Croatia, 120 miles south east of Split. The old city has double ramparts with 20 towers and bastions. There is a Baroque Cathedral and some exquisite churches. Waking early we found we were already at anchor in Dubrovnik. We were first off, by tender, to the pier near to the centre of town to go on a tour. The first photo stop was predictable and we jostled with a number of other coaches to park in the restricted layby to get the panoramic views of the town. Then a climb, in the bus not on foot, took us to another view where we could see Dubrovnik, Minerva and the island which has many rare and exotic plants given over the years by plant collectors. The Konavle valley below is a wide fertile valley with three rivers and a climate that allows the cultivation of citrus fruit, apples, vines and vegetables, though vast tracts seemed to be left fallow. Our stop was at a delightful restaurant, the Konavoski Dvori. Tables were under striped canopies in the shade of trees, set with white cloths, cutlery and glasses.

We were served by waitresses in traditional costumes, with bread, ham and cheese, all local produce made using long-practised methods. To drink, there was a choice of red or white wine, all from the local vineyards. All this at 9.30 in the morning. One could, of course, have chosen a soft drink or water! There was then the inevitable trip to the 'outside' toilets, which were immaculate! The surroundings were beautiful with streams running through the site, weirs, little channelled canals and working waterwheels.

The coach then took us to the village of Cavtat where we enjoyed the walk between the lakeside and the cafes along the promenade. We retraced our steps after a short sit looking out over the sea before getting back onto the coach. The return to Dubrovnik went without incident and we caught the tender in the nick of time before it left for the ship. Since our outward transfer the sea had become very choppy and getting into the side of Minerva was tricky but nothing like as tricky as getting the passengers off and onto the steps. We were virtually thrown up in moments of calm. It was interesting watching subsequent transfers as the swell got worse.

As it was Sunday the restaurant and Veranda were serving an excellent Sunday roast which Derek much enjoyed. We spent the afternoon on our balcony, having decided not to return to Dubrovnik by tender, we didn't fancy the crowds. Instead we watched the canoeists, the sailing boats and the "pirate" ship passing to and fro, with an interval for afternoon tea. At 6.30 we went to the church service; a very Anglican communion, and a very amusing address by Victor Stock.

Dinner had the choice of the buffet or the delicious pasta dishes cooked and served outside on the veranda. These options gave sufficient nutrients to tackle the quiz! We made up our six with Mike and Eileen and Keith and Heather; they proved a very pleasant foursome and we spent a lot of time with them subsequently. In the quiz tonight we came second!! No-one was happy with that but decided the next quiz would have a different outcome.

And so we went on to Sibenik, first settled by the Croats and conquered by the Venetians in 1116. It then passed between various kingdoms until falling to the Venetians in 1412. They ruled until 1797 when it passed to the Austrian empire until 1918. In WW1 the Italians occupied it, and then it became part of the Serbs, Croats and Slovene Kingdom. This lasted till the Yugoslav army shelled the town in 1991. It was liberated by the Croatian army in Operation Storm in 1995. The fierce fighting destroyed not only much of the town but the aluminium industry as well.

Derek was originally going on the town tour but decided against it because of the distance to walk just to get to the centre.

Barbara went on the trip to Krka national park.. The start of the trip was interesting and most un-Minerva like. There had been a muddle in the issuing of tickets, in that those on the wait-list had tickets saying 'reserve' which they took to mean reserved seats and not that they would get onto the trip if there was room. This led to several heated disputes on the quay side and a lot of ill feeling. Eventually everyone was allowed on the coaches, which were therefore very full

It was an interesting drive to Skradin across the wide plain with olives groves and sweeps of pines. The town itself was a sleepy little place on the river Krka and in the tourist literature "renowned for its gastronomy". So we looked forward to our drink and snack. We got to the café where chaos reigned. There were far more people than the café was expecting. There were too few seats; only one (harassed and grumpy) waitress; no snacks and a long wait for orange juice, that wasn't worth it anyway, So Barbara preferred to wander through the streets of the town. It was really quiet but pleasant with an interesting church. All the streets led to the harbour/marina with its shops selling all the usual seaside tack. In the marina there were splendid, vastly expensive yachts, including, apparently one belonging to Abramovitch. The harbour and its immediate surroundings was named by Bill Gates as his favourite vacation place.

The guides then gave us confusing instructions. "Everyone go to the queue for the boat", "Group One go there"; "Group

Two wait here" It didn't help that we had no idea which group we were in. In the end we all just queued up, got on the boat and most of us managed to get a spot on the top. It was a lovely gentle half hour trip along the river Krka between the densely wooded hills and the low lying swamp areas where there were swans and cormorants. Too soon we arrived at Skradinski Buk, the quay to get to the waterfalls.

These have formed because of the barriers of travertine, a deposit of calcium carbonate, which forms on moss and continues to grow due to the ongoing absorption of the calcium and carbon; as a result the barriers grow and change by 1-2mm each year altering the flow of the streams and waterfalls.

After a slight delay to get the tickets we were directed to the visitor centre with usual 'amenities', a few souvenir and hot dog stalls and ice cream vendors. Then we went across the river on a foot bridge, which led to a path on the opposite side which had the best views of the main cascades of the Krka waterfalls so the photographers were lined up jostling for the best spot The falls were magnificent and the spray from them travelled a long way, as far as those standing on the bridge who therefore got wet; it was quite exhilarating and not unpleasant. We climbed the steps to the boardwalk to a beautiful walk through the woods, over little bridges and all the way walking alongside or over small waterfalls. It was possible to pause and look at the pools and listen to the water rippling along. There were tiny islands created by the meandering of the river, trees and plants. It was a treat to enjoy the atmosphere.

Too soon I was at the end of the walk and at a point where there were more toilets, souvenir shops and a café. We eventually found the bus. and sat with a pleasant chatty man, from Lancashire, who thought were his friends for the rest of the voyage.

We were back late so we decided not to walk into Sibenik but to enjoy the balcony instead after a BBQ lunch on deck. There was a themed dinner again on veranda, this time it was an Asian stir fry night, very good and very spicy by European standards! Later in the evening Lynda Chang, the other half of 'Linda Snell', gave a piano recital of classical music.

Next day we were in Pula. The gentle walking group to visit Pula set off at the civilised time of 9.15 to meet our, very English guide, Graham. He was good but with far too much information. Pula today is the main administrative centre of of an area of Croatia but feeling different from the other places we visited. The Romans ruled Istria from 177 BC, hence all the significant Roman remains but there is still an Italian feel to the town; from 1856 Pula passed from the Austrian domination to the Italians and it was heavily bombed by the allies in WW11. Italian was the official language for many years and is still spoken by much of the population today.

However we were to visit the nearby spectacular amphitheatre known locally as the Arena. The amphitheatre was very close to the berth so within minutes we were approaching the entrance but before that we passed a rather nice statue to all sailors lost in both world wars.

The arena was certainly an impressive building with three storeys of arches still standing from 27BC when its construction started; it was finished in 68AD. The outside is original but parts of the interior have been restored over the years. New walls and seats have been put in so that it can host the festivals, for which it is famous. It is one of only seven complete amphitheatres in the world and as the guide listed them we realised we had now seen six of them, just a Spanish one to go.

The undercroft proved most interesting especially the fourth century map of Europe, an intriguing interpretation by the map makers of the time as to where countries were and how big they were. More predictable were the amphora and the olive presses.

Our gentle walk then complete, we walked slowly round part of the old town. We saw the cathedral of the Assumption, built on the foundations of a Roman Temple in the 4th century but much enlarged from the single nave church which it was then. A little further on we saw the impressive Temple of Augustus. We made it as far as the town hall and the town hall square, which was pleasant. We had hoped to walk up to the Franciscan chapel, which was impressive apparently, but the hill and the uneven terrain put us off. So we made our way back, slowly, along the sea side, which was interesting with its variety of boats, but a long way.

An excellent curry lunch, prepared by the Maître d no less, revived our energies, so we set off again to look at the Triumphal Arch of Sergii but the uneven cobbled streets put us off going too far. As ever the street café scene entertained us. Barbara even had enough energy to go to the craft session to renew her limited skills of crochet.

The next day the alarm went at 6 a.m. for us to watch the entry into Venice. The run in was magical, at first it was quite dark but the buildings were lit beautifully, some inside and some outside and some both. There were churches, palaces, some houses, domes and bell towers. Most spectacular was the run past the Doges Palace, the campanile of St. Mark and the entrance to St. Mark's Square. The sail in was enhanced by an excellent deck talk from Prof Andrew Hopkins.

We nearly lost our guide on the way to the boat that was to take us to Murano; she walked too briskly for us and several others and it didn't help that there were no Minerva staff at the tricky turnings

Our sail on a small boat was damp and misty so many of the sights were seen only vaguely. We did however see the 1890 flour mill that milled the flour that came from Russia, which it is now a five star hotel. The island opposite was once a prison island but only for the rich criminals, the poor suffered the terrible prison conditions nearer the centre of Venice. We crossed St. Mark's pool leaving St. Mark's cathedral and the Ducal Palace behind. St. George's Island is now a marina, no longer a convent and monastery. The Pianale gardens were established by Napoleon and were full of trees and plants "to increase the oxygen". They now house the Art Biennale.

We passed many bridges; apparently there are 403 in Venice. There are also many individual islands some of which were identified; the one with the international university; the Lido, which forms a unique barrier between the Lagoon and the Adriatic; a fortified island housing the Swiss solar boat, the island of St. Peter whose church is the only one with a white stone bell tower, the Arsenal which once had 16,000 boat builders who could build a boat in a day (a feat also attributed to the British); the cemetery island well away from the rest of the city and finally Murano emerged from the mist.

We disembarked at the quay for the Furnace Estavan Rossetto to watch the remarkable and extremely hot skill of glass blowing. The, corpulent, men carried large amounts of molten glass around the factory periodically feeding them into ridiculously hot furnaces and then manipulating, rolling and blowing it into figures, vases, lights and animals. We were standing in front of one of the furnaces and even from a safe distance behind the rope barrier it was seriously hot!

At the end of the demonstrations we were, of course, shepherded into the showrooms and shops. As we did not wish to buy any glass, at exorbitant prices, we strolled along the quay beside the canal, the boats and the scavenging gulls and then turned and retraced our steps through a pretty arch to a café where we were deciding if we had time for a drink. At this point Derek was hailed! It turned out that it was an ex-clerk from Stockport court who had had a lot to do with Derek when he was a magistrate.

Even more to our astonishment, they were also on Minerva! Later in the cruise we had a very pleasant afternoon tea with him, Phil, and his wife An hour later, having sailed through more islands, Torcello appeared through the thickening mist. Torcello was invaded and occupied by the Romans and then the Venetians and grew into an important political and trading centre from the 10th century. The lagoon and the salt marshes helped in the development of Torcello but also in its demise as the swamps became home to the mosquitos that brought malaria.

Getting off the boat we started the walk, described as long in the cruise book, which was really quite pleasant. We passed small fields and what we would call allotments on one side and a little canal on the other. It was crossed by small, steep bridges; one especially was very steep and called, locally, the devil's little bridge. There were also one or two nice looking cafes. We made a note of them for the way back.

At the end of the path was the Cathedral Santa Maria Assunta famous for its Byzantine mosaics. It was founded in 639 as a simple, single nave chapel but over the centuries it has been much changed with many renovations.

In the apse is a big mosaic of the Virgin against a gold background above a row of standing Apostles, dating from the 11th century. On the opposite west wall was an even bigger mosaic with many scenes including, at the top, the Crucifixion and four more layers with all manner of Biblical scenes, one of which one stood out – the gruesome depiction of the Last Judgement. Both mosaics were beautifully done, We emerged from the cathedral into heavy rain so we couldn't appreciate the 11th-century Church of Santa Fosca standing next to the cathedral and notable for its five sided portico in the form of a Greek cross. We were actually sheltering under a tiny canopy outside the museum of Torcello which is housed in the original 14 th century palaces. It also housed the inevitable souvenir shop which sold an excellent guide book.

However, by now the rain was pelting down and everyone else seemed to be making their way back to the boat, so we didn't have time for anymore photos, coffee or any appreciation of the lovely, tranquil, wet, island. We were last on board, literally soaked to the skin. The inside of the boat was festooned with wet garments, to say nothing of wet passengers. The condensation on the windows obscured any views there might have been. The driver of the boat even tried to warm us up with the heater, but it was a losing battle. We eventually got back to Minerva and after a complete change of clothes went along to Veranda for a buffet Italian lunch.

We had intended to go into Venice during the afternoon but the weather and the thought of negotiating the motor taxis put us off and instead we watched the life on the lagoon and succumbed to afternoon tea.

The next day we were in Ravenna, which we had hoped would be one of the special days of the cruise and the main reason we had chosen it. It certainly lived up to our expectations.

We docked at 8 a.m. and were off on the coach transfer to Ravenna itself half-an-hour later, which took about 20 minutes. We were berthed in the passenger dock so we were near beaches, which looked lovely, and the marina full of yachts as well as small craft. The centre was 11 kilometres from the port and the land we travelled over was reclaimed from the sea. The road ran alongside the canal that once took quite big boats right into the centre of Ravenna. On each side were the estuarine salt marshes and all along the length of the waterway were small fishing cottages and huge fishing nets which were hauled up out of the canal when we drove past. We spotted several heron and egrets. On the opposite side of the road was a large petrochemical centre. In the distance we could see a second port, a commercial one which imported cereal from Russia and distributed it to Ravenna and the surrounding area.

As we got nearer into town we stopped to view Theodric's Mausoleum. It was quite a sight built of great grey blocks of Istrian stone cut from Istrian rocks and carried across the Adriatic. It was topped by a fine white dome and had been built on the orders of Theodoric in the 500s to show his importance and power as a Roman Emperor. It has two floors; the lower has graves of the more ordinary mortals and the upper one the tombs of the nobles. The surrounding cemetery was created on land reclaimed from the marshes. In the distance were a number of pine trees, the remnants of a forest. Pines were important as timber for houses and for the pine nuts they produced.

On the last part of the run into Ravenna the road was lined with colleges teaching the art of restoration and conservation of the mosaics, obviously a big part of the employment in the area. The dropping off point was Piazza Barraca; the name of the square was repeated to us several times because this was where we had to meet after our tour and enjoy free time. We all remembered the Piazza but how to retrace our steps to get there was another matter.

We set off for the 6th-century basilica of St. Vitale, through the grand white Roman arch and into the church itself which was constructed so the entrance was dark but you walked into the light as you entered the Basilica, and it really was like that. Even the decoration of black and white tiles on the floor was arranged so that they led you into the fabulous apse along a route that conveyed the sense of having to walk a hard route to gain salvation and "the light". A bit flowery but somehow it rang true. Around the apse were eight pillars which supported the dome and allowed small galleries set aside for the women and reserved for their prayer.

The dome had a mosaic showing Christ as the Redeemer, sitting on the globe and with the roll of the seven seals. He has an angel on each side of Him; on the right St. Vitale to whom he offers the martyr's crown and on the left a bishop who offers a model of the church to Christ. At their feet is the garden and above them a golden sky decorated with coloured clouds – just one of the wonderful mosaic pictures. The walls were decorated with frescoes; the capitals of the pillars were shaped like baskets and sculpted with lotus leaves and the marble of the pillars had veining that set off the rest of the amazing decoration and mosaics.

We went a little further into the Presbytery which had the most fantastic mosaics; too many to describe them all, but those we were most impressed by were: : the small roundel of Christ between the lunettes (semi circles below the dome) surrounded by green intertwined dolphins; lots of Old Testament stories, such as the sacrifices by Abel, Moses leading a flock of sheep and going into an oak wood on fire (!?) ; tmany stories associated with Abraham; images of Empresses, Theodora; Emperors; Justinian; lots of angels; many apostles; beautiful depictions of Jerusalem and Bethlehem but above all (for me) gorgeous animals, everything from donkeys to ducks, lions to sheep, doves, peacocks, herons… and more, and on every picture flowers, plants, stars, puddles and reeds.

We were overwhelmed and went back in the afternoon to look again but would still like to return one day.

An intriguing scenario took place behind us where two or three conservation students were assessing the state of the tiled floor which is gradually sinking as the water table gets lower. The students are mapping the whole floor, tile by tile, before assessing the state of each one. This involved kneeling down and tapping each of the square tiles with a small hammer and listening intently to distinguish between the sound of a tile that is unstable and therefore needs resetting and one that had a firm base. They were delightful young people and willing to talk to us and explain what they were doing and how they would conserve the tiled floor.

It was time for our group to move on; given the number of visitors times into the attractions had to be limited (because of the moisture and carbon dioxide breathed out) and carefully controlled. Our next stop was the deceptively simple Mausoleum of Galla Placida, outside quite plain but inside is breath taking. Perhaps it was because there was only a few of us and we could go in quietly and enter through the barrel shaped vault which was quite dark but then the interior was magnificent and lit by the light from the arched windows. The dome of the entrance is deep blue and decorated in gold and covered in "moons" holding red and white flowers.

Moving further in and looking up we could see the dome with a gold cross in the centre of a vivid blue starry sky. At each of four corners with the symbols of the four evangelists; Mark's lion; Luke's ox; John's eagle and the man of Matthew. They seemed to be flying in towards the cross.

There were lunettes round the mausoleum one depicting Paul and Peter in white tunics; Paul holds a scroll and Peter his key; below them, at their feet, doves drinking from a vessel or a fountain. In other lunettes deer beautifully executed with their typical marking and antlers and wrapped round with Agapanthus stems. Turning to look back at the entrance and over the door, there was the Good Shepherd, a young man without a beard, welcoming small sheep into paradise sitting on a field of grass and flowers.

Above the sarcophagus, supposedly that of Gallia Placida, the mosaic shows St. Lawrence about to be burnt on a grill carrying a martyr's cross (the flames actually look like red worms!). On the floor on the left there is a cabinet with its doors open showing the four gospels, a powerful picture.

Our time was up so we emerged to the sunlight and being given free time. obviously that suggested coffee but by the time we got to the first café it was already full of 'swans' so on to the next and we got a seat outside. However the service was so chaotic and took so long we used their facilities and then abandoned the wait for coffee, had a short wander and then went back to the allotted square to pick up the coach with Heather and Keith who, luckily were confident of the direction we had to take.

We drove to the 6th century church San Apollinare in Classe on our way back to the ship. We had hoped it would be St. Apollinaire in Novo as that seemed to have wonderful mosaics but it wasn't to be. The church was out of town, standing in cultivated fields on a great plain between Ravenna and Rimini. There were five life size bullocks in bronze, all with a really life like pose; so much so that Keith insisted on "feeding" them and had his picture taken to prove it. The outside of the church is built of pinkish brick and is really nice with its arched mullion windows and slim white columns. To the left of the main doorway is the10th century bell tower constructed of red and yellow bricks set in diamond patterns. The tower has four sets of mullion windows and a shallow dome on the top. It was saved in WW11 from both the German mines, set as the troops retreated, and bombing by the allies. It came under the threat of attack because it was used by the German army as an observation point.

The interior was breathtakingly beautiful; it was so light and so tall and with a high wooden roof. The light came in through the ground floor windows but also through the mullion windows high on the side walls, under the roof beams. The twenty four columns on each side of the nave led the eye to the apse and its wonderful dome. Each of the columns was of green and white veined marble, somehow totally in keeping the mosaic scenes in the apse. The capitals were decorated with acanthus leaves and open fretwork. Above the columns were frescoes of the bishops of Ravenna.

As we walked into the nave we were immediately taken by its size and grandeur but then by an enormous piece of modern art in the form of a sort of flat pyramid or 3D triangle. surrounded by dozens of little golden ships "sailing" on their own sea of rice! Not quite sure of the significance, but it was spectacular.

The dome in the apse was exquisite; the first feature you see is the large gold jewelled cross with the face of Christ in the middle, it is set in a sky of blue with 99 gold and silver stars (reference to the 99 sheep?); above the cross is the hand of God appearing from the clouds (reference to the transfiguration) and on each side the figures of the great prophets Elijah and Moses. Beneath are three lambs representing Peter, James and John as well as palm trees which represent the sign of Martyrdom.

The lowest scene is perhaps the most beautiful, a real pastoral scene with birds, flowers, trees and grass making up the 'mystical lawn'! There are 12 sheep walking along, (the 12 apostles) and in the very centre, and the largest figure in the mosaic, St. Apollinare. Our time was nearly up but there was the last chance to walk back up the nave to admire the detail in the carvings on the ancient coffins.

We had a leisurely lunch before taking the shuttle service back into the town. We revisited the cathedral and then made our way, gently, along the main street, laid with polished tiles, so it was easy walking except for the numerous cyclists who took no prisoners. We continued through the town square to Via a Diaz. By this time we were wondering if we would get to the Baptistery that had been so recommended to us. We had to turn down a little, unnamed, street, go to the end and turn right and a short distance along the Baptistery emerges in the most unlikely looking little square.

It was a tiny, octagonal Byzantine church that had been part of another much larger church, now gone. Other building had gone on for centuries, so the Baptistery is partly buried. We went down a few steps, after waiting for another couple to emerge; there was room for only two or three inside. It was quite dark with little apses and small arched openings that didn't let much light in however you could put on a timed switch to see the beautiful mosaic dome.

The main subject was the baptism of Jesus by John. Jesus is young and beardless, he is naked (and the explicit nature of his nakedness may explain some of the reputation of this tiny chapel) and partly submerged in the River Jordan. On one side, John wears a leopard skin and on the other a white haired old man with a green cloak; he represents a pagan god of the river. Above Jesus is the Holy Spirit in the form of a white dove spitting water from its beak Below the baptism is a procession of Apostles who meet at a throne bearing a crucifix on a purple cushion. We could see that the green mosaic grass the apostles walk on is made of different coloured stones indicating that the mosaic had been worked on for a number of years.

We were glad we had made the effort to find the baptistery, but It was time to retrace our steps through the town hall square looking for a café when we spotted a little café hidden away in a courtyard. It was delightful and after gesticulations and broken English and Italian we got a beer each and a piece of cake to share. Cold beerm, tasty cake and a sit in the sunshine people-watching – couldn't be better

We got the second, and last, shuttle back to the ship half an hour before departure time, just in time to hear the amusing 'lecture' by Victor Stock. The sail from Ravenna was in the evening sun, taking on board the pilot and passing the marina full of yachts.

After dinner there was another performance by Cadenza with both Carol Boyd and the pianist Lynda Chang on "The

English in Love" – another excellent entertainment and very funny.

The next day was very normal day at sea, pleasant with lots to do if one chose to and plenty to eat. There wasn't a long lie in as the first lecture was at 9.00 followed by a craft workshop which was crochet. That was great because Barbara wanted to remember how to do it, like a number of others, though Karin did say later we were a bit slow reconnecting to the technique.

Lunch followed, out on the veranda. balcony and passing scenery was too tempting and, of course, there was afternoon tea Derek went to the later lecture and we both went to dinner

The evening finished with the excellent crew show, some very familiar acts and some new ones, all appreciated by the passengers.

The following day we were revisiting Alberobello the unusual and special little town near Brindisi. The country side was interesting and the guide both instructive and amusing at times with her pronunciation. She told us about the founding of Brindisi in the 7th century BC, and how it became important to the Romans from the 1st century BC. Apulia has one of the longest coastlines and with flat land behind it, it was easily invaded. The French were one of the conquerors and to this day there is a strong influence of the French language with many familiar words.

Apulia means without water and it has 300 days of sunshine. This affects the agriculture of the area; we passed fields, some ploughed, and some fallow. though very few cattle anywhere but lots of poly tunnels, which make it easier to irrigate the crop and to retain the water. Scattered among the fields were lonely farm houses, mostly square and single storey, surrounded by their barns. All the buildings were white in the village as well as the farms are painted with lime twice a year. This tradition started in the middle ages when the people believed it kept the Black Death away. It continues today as it is recognised that lime has some antibacterial properties. It also "helps to push the sun away."

As we began to climb from the plain we could see in the distance ancient cave settlements in the rocks as well as cisterns and the occasional church. The fields began to be divided up by dry stone walls to create terraces for olive groves and vineyards. Some of the olive trees on the edges of the fields were huge and reputed to be more than 1000 years old. The wine from Apulia has a high reputation and 40% of Italian wine comes from the region with the white wine being especially famous.

Nearer to Alberobello the nature of the farmhouses changed and they were strongly fortified with high stone walls surrounding all the buildings. The crops cultivated changed to cherry orchards and almond groves. We drove first on the outskirts of the modern city and then to the famous 15th century village. No traffic is allowed inside so there were shuttle buses waiting for those with limited mobility.

The houses are the trulli, built of local limestone using the dry stone method; there was no water or cement at all. They are round and the roof is conical with a keystone otherwise the roof would collapse, and at the top is the chimney. Many of the trulli have white markings on them some are religious, some magical and some just pretty. The method of building was designed so that the roof could be instantly dismantled therefore the house couldn't be lived in, so it wasn't a house, therefore they avoided the tax man.

Today most of the trulli are little shops selling souvenirs, model trulli and pasta (Some of the trulli have persuasive owners standing outside trying to get visitors to go inside and see the interior, the furnishings and the panoramic views and then to taste the wine. After that the hard sell starts.

Very few trulli are lived in as homes, they are too small, have no garden, yard or garage but a few have been knocked together to provide a more modern home. At the top of the hill is the church of St. Anthony; The outside is trulli style but inside it is very modern, light and white with a modern apse painted with angels, monks, peacocks and a large central crucifix set in the midst of branches and leaves. At one side is a modern, large model of St. Anthony of Padua, patron saint of the church.

 We continued slowly down the hill admiring the side streets decorated with window boxes and containers of flowers; a displays of chillies, souvenir shops and the multi coloured pasta. By the time we were at the bottom it was coffee time. We passed the first café, full of swans, and opted for the next where coffee and chocolate were bought. Barbara left Derek sitting at the table and climbed the hill opposite to capture the panorama from a high vantage point.

We decided to walk back to the coach rather than wait for the shuttle and were back comfortably before the shuttle and in good time for the coach to take us back to Minerva. Lunch was again on the deck of veranda, we were, by now dab hands at getting ahead of the crowd to bag an outside table and while one kept guard the other could return to the cabin if necessary. Today there were delicious baked potatoes on offer with all manner of fillings and salads. Great!

In the afternoon we decided to explore Brindisi which looked attractive from the ship. We borrowed a map and took advice from Heather and Keith who had gone earlier. The sky looked a bit dark but we were optimistic and set off with one umbrella. Via Garibaldi was a wide, tree lined boulevard with posh shops, all closed; we thought we were following the map but took a wrong turn and ended up near the market square. It was then large spots of rain came down and within seconds it was pouring There was no shelter except for a tiny awning over a delicatessen and butcher shop.

We thought that as the rain started so suddenly it would stop as suddenly. It didn't and we stood under the canopy getting wetter. It was then the owner took pity on us and insisted we stood inside and he went and got a chair for Derek. While he continued to clean the shop, they had clearly shut some time previously. We tried to converse with our limited Italian and he his even more limited English. His wife, hearing this strange conversation came out, duster in hand and proceeded to wipe imaginary spots off the counter.

Eventually we felt we had overstayed our welcome and even though it was still pouring we managed to get an idea of where we were and how to get back to the ship. The streets were now rivers of water, the downspouts were waterfalls and the drains overwhelmed. We had to keep crossing from side to side to avoid the worst of the pools of water, even so we were wet! Eventually we got back to the Via Garibaldi, having passed several groups of fellow passengers sheltering in a variety of shop doorways, and then to the ship.

We were drenched to the skin and needed a complete change of clothes before afternoon tea. The laundrette and its dryers had a busy few hours and our shower looked like a bad drying day!

We left our berth at 5 o'clock and watched the coast line as we sailed, failing to identify the very tall monument though we think it was built to commemorate the sailors lost in various conflicts. Dinner, however, was very pleasant with our fellow quizzers. Everyone was delighted to be joint winners of the quiz, especially as we then shared a bottle of bubbly. The stopper of the bottle became the team trophy and was duly shared around the team. It remains in the safe keeping of Keith.

We had a bit of a bumpy night; the sea was bumpy as well as our sleep and we managed to sleep late and miss the church service; a pity because Victor Stock was amusing last time, but his way of conducting communion wasn't ours! We also opted out of the first lecture but went to the second by Victor, not that the content had much to do with the title but it was entertaining.

Lunch was again a BBQ and the weather was calm now so lunch could be taken! The afternoon passed watching the sea go by and reading, until afternoon tea and waffles, with ice cream!

About 6 p.m. we went out onto the deck to watch, and to hear the deck talk, as we traversed the Straits of Messina between the eastern tip of Sicily and the western point of Calabria. Luckily the sea was more or less calm; apparently it has been known to be choppy going through the straits as there are strong tidal currents. The sky ahead was almost black and we could see fork lightning and hear the rumble of thunder, however we avoided the storm. On the left we passed one of the tallest pylons in the world, the Torre Faro, which used to carry the overhead power line, which is now beneath the sea but the pylons have protected status and remain.

We had a pleasant dinner with Mike and Eileen, our quiz companions and duly, and with ceremony, exchanged the 'trophy'. Sometime after 10pm we drew abreast of Stromboli and were treated to a pyrotechnic display. It is one of the most active volcanos in the world with small regular eruptions; has given rise to the name "Lighthouse of the Mediterranean". Tonight Stromboli had its head in the clouds so we couldn't see the eruptions except as a red glow in the cloud. The lava flows were pretty spectacular and we felt a certain concern for the villages at the foot of the volcano on the coast. We had enjoyed a different show"from Stromboli when we went round it on *Spirit of Adventure* but it was interesting to see the lava flows against the night sky.

Next day we cruised up the west coast of Italy this morning and it was so nice we abandoned packing and sat on the balcony until coffee time and "The cruise in retrospect", which was interesting and amusing as each of the lecturers spoke.

After an early lunch we set off in the tender for the town of Gaeta. We knew nothing about it except what the Minerva handbook said. "A fishing and oil seaport and a renowned tourist resort"; the tourist board web site described it as "a gorgeous place which can find its origins in Ancient Rome; its narrow alleys and huge castle are medieval it has lovely and relaxing beaches".

Unfortunately we didn't appreciate any of these sentiments. so set off walking along the front but then branched off up the side of a shady square into a pleasant street of modern apartments with their own balconies. This led us to the cathedral but it was closed. A little further on was another church we had hoped to look in but it too was closed, as was the museum. This meant we were rather at a loss as to what to do but round the corner we found a café patronised by a number of other Swans looking for refuge. It was a pleasant spot; it served a good beer and we could look at the harbour one way and the fine bell tower of the cathedral the other.

The capital of the bell tower, visible from a large part of the town, stands at 57 metres and was beautiful. It was built with many Roman remains but its top was the most spectacular. The square section was decorated with tiny white pillars holding the Romanesque arches and above that an octagonal section with round towers on four corners and windows on each part divided into two smaller arched windows Right at the top another octagonal layer with more pillars supporting the last delicate hexagonal 'crown'. The small bricks of the tower were in white and cream, the decoration was of majolica with lots of blue. It looked as though it had recently been restored as the colours were so bright.

When we had finished our drinks we went for a stroll further along the street and came across a beautiful little

Byzantine chapel, almost perfect in its construction but woefully neglected. It was the church of San Giovanni Mare and dates from the 10th century. Its door was partly barricaded but it was possible to still see inside. There was a simple cross in what would have been the apse, a plain altar, some frescoes in the side chapels and a short nave supported by three columns whose capitals had the remains of nice carving. The rest of the chapel was damp and the decoration was flaking off. It was sad and somehow typified the rest of the old town, as we had experienced it.

We made our way back to the tender in a slightly subdued mood; Gaeta had not been what we expected. Spirits were raised by the prospect of a Viennese special afternoon tea.

In the evening we had the farewell gala dinner. It was very good especially as we sat with our quizzer companions.

The next day was Inevitably a long one: we were one of the last groups to leave as we were on a late flight to Gatwick. At least it was fine and warm and there were loungers to lie on to read our books, and Minerva provided a very acceptable lunch. We had a long wearying journey ahead of us as we we were flying into Gatwick, late, and couldn't connect with a Heathrow flight to Manchester that evening so we had to stay at the Sofitel at Heathrow which involved getting the coach between the two airports. However the assistance, in Rome airport, was very good; after being "corralled" in the assistance waiting area we were taken through security briskly, on to a buggy and up to the lounge where we had a drink and snacks. We encountered our ex-neighbour, Norma, who was having trouble claiming her right to be in the business lounge. It turned out she wasn't supposed to be there, Cynthia had only booked business for them on the outward journey, but she managed to stay.

The flight was fine and we were fed but then there was the case to retrieve from the carousel and the shuttle bus stop to find The driver loaded the case into the boot and we were off along the M25 to Heathrow. It was an interesting transfer, especially as we didn't have to drive.

There was the usual long trek to the hotel but it was very comfortable when we got there. We, as usual, bought provisions from M&S in the terminal, saved one little bottle of wine from the aircraft so we had supper before retiring to bed.

The next day we went home. We had our breakfast in the lounge and were picked up to be taken to the gate. The flight as ever and the assistance in Manchester was incredible. The young man arrived with a wheel chair, collected the case from the carousel, carried it and pushed the wheel chair all the way to the car. Barbara went to get the key from Meet & Greet, he loaded the case into the boot and he was off before we had time to give him, a well-deserved, tip.

All that remained now was to collect the dog on the way home, unpack and do the washing!

A very good cruise with excellent companions…until!

Notable Fellow Passengers

Keith, ex-pilot and lots of other things and Heather, retired primary head, a cancer sufferer,Hertfordshire – and quizzers.

Eileen (a PA, still working) and Mike (with a grandson starting at Chester University).
Norma and Cynthia – cabin next door.

Pam (from Norwich, worked for Colmans and Janet Ipswich.

Peter and Julie, both artists from Tunbridge Wells).

Emma, Canadian, her mother, Bridget, a Conservative councillor, and Christopher and partner on the table for six.

Dorothy (sat next to her on waterfall trip) and her friend Jennifer.

Chapter 8

Russia by River: From Moscow to St Petersburg

For our visit to Russia in 1996 our arrangements were made by the Noble Caledonia company, travelling via Vienna, where we stayed for three days en route to Moscow and our Russia story starts when we arrived in Moscow Airport to join a long queue to go through the rather intimidating customs control, but we eventually got through and were assembled by Tom of Noble Caledonia, who checked that we were all there and had identified our luggage, which would now be taken to the ship separately from us. We boarded a coach to go to North Dock where our ship the MS Yesinin was waiting. We were shown to our cabins. Ours (number 130) was not quite finished, but it was clear in a few minutes, by which time our bags had arrived, so we unpacked, settled in and had a short stroll along the quay, returning to get ready at 7.00 p.m for dinner.

Next day we are about to start seeing Moscow, so some introductory notes: it is no longer the capital of a communist state, but the capital of a country with a long history, having been founded by Prince Yuri Dolgorikiy in 1157. We collected our packed lunches and boarded the coach and drove along wide streets which became increasingly congested. We passed some rather austere and characterless buildings from the communist era, interspersed with small houses, palaces and exquisite churches, now being opened up after the end of the soviet period.

Our first stop is on Sparrow Hill, where the Mathematics faculty of Moscow university is located, and providing superb views across the city below. Then we go down to tour the Kremlin, which we expected to be grim and dour, but was actually magnificent. We went first through the Armoury with embroidered regalia from the period of the Czar,s. horse decorations, jewels, Sevres porcelain, crowns, state coaches and five of the famous Faberge eggs, the only others are in the USA. to eat our sandwich lunches we were taken to an old cinema on the outskirts of the city, where we were offered free vodka!!

Our next visit was to Gorki park with the dramatic and sobering monument commemorating 50 years since the end of World War 2, including representations of concentration camps, including personal items abandoned by people on the way to the gas chambers. We then moved on to Red Square, dominated by St Basil's Cathedral ad it's distinctive onion-shaped domes alongside Lenin's tomb set in the wall of the Kremlin.

On another side of the square was the completely unexpected and amazing GUM at the time we were there it was the only one in Russia and GUM was an abbreviation of Main Universal Store. Today it is known as State Department Store, carrying 106 different brands, as well as cafes and restaurants. It was very, very big but austere. Barbara's note at the time was, "A bit like a wrought-iron Covent Garden."

On our way back to the ship, we went via the Metro stations, which were opulent, decorated and all different with frequent trains that were crowded and noisy.

It is worth providing a summary of the menu for dinner that evening: stuffed tomatoes with coleslaw, a piece of beef with spaghetti, tinned cold peas and cold pickled pepper, a bun and coffee, all washed down by ample red wine, which an American couple, Lou and Jan, described as "like Concorde wine".

Next day after breakfast we set off to go to Red square by metro, counting the number of stations, so that we could count them back when we returned to the ship. It turned out that Red square was closed as Lenin's tomb was open and you had to go through special checks and leave cameras behind, so we didn't bother, but walked round side streets instead and heard a military band and some orthodox priests celebrating something we did't understand.

Returning by metro was easy, although Jill's husband was nearly robbed by two gypsies with babies in slings on their backs, but he quickly caught them and sent them off. Back at the ship, we pottered round the local market and bought some fruit, with the total to pay being added up using an abacus.

Lunch was very substantial, so we walked along the quay for a while until we could see the beginning of miles of conifer forests before going back to our cabin for a nice relaxing afternoon to unwind. 6.30 was the Captain's cocktail party with plentiful Vodka and Champagne. For the Excellent Welcome dinner we sat with Rosie and Peter, who was very good at acquiring an extra bottle of champagne.

*　　*　　*

Next day we had emergency drill on deck as we all put on our life jackets and went through the drill as required. we also had a talk about the lock system before an early lunch at 12 noon. At 1.30 we arrived at Uglich, where we were the third ship to arrive ad were double berthed and walked through another ship to disembark to a musician with an accordion and a girl with a loaf of bread from which we broke off a piece and dipped it in salt a traditional Russian greeting. We had only a short stay in Uglich as the ship was due to sail again at 5.p.m.

We went first to the cathedral of the transfiguration, now a museum, where a group of novice monks sang anthems for us quite wonderfully with mainly bass voices. From here to the Church of Saint Dimitri-on-the-blood, a tiny wooden building. Inside there were fine frescoes telling the history of how Dimitri was murdered. Outside we decided it was not an attractive stop as the people seemed to be down trodden and down and out. Boy of about 15 passed us stumbling along with a small handful of Kopecks that he was dropping as he staggered. he was followed by (presumably) his grandmother trying to pick them up for him, and then he was violently sick.

We were glad to be back on the ship, and we had a pleasant sit in the observation lounge as we cruised across a reservoir and eventually on to Mother Volga. Before dinner there was a performance by a folk group of girls, singing ad dancing with more enthusiasm than professionalism, although they did manage to get Derek to participate!

Next day we were cruising the Volga towards Kostrama and

an early lunch before disembarking and boarding coaches to drive up the hill to the nineteenth century centre of the town. There were many derelict factories and 20%unemployment, according to our guide, caused by capitalism. We also toured the Patievsky monastery and heard the singing of a girls choir, one of whom had a remarkable voice. Then we moved to the open-air museum of wooden architecture. t had a variety of items gathered together from the local area: wooden houses, wells, windmills, barns and boat houses. There were also some exquisite examples of weaving and embroidery.

Nearby we were able to visit an active nunnery, recently returned to the Church, with a startling white iconostasis with a sacred Icon of Virgin and Child, but now blank because a restorer damaged it with his knife, and it turned black overnight! Then it was back on the coach to drive up to the town square to wander round the stalls, including a souvenir shop where we bought a small lacquered container. Then we walked back to the ship for dinner, and then to bed as the ship moved of towards our next destination of Yaroslav, although we apparently stop once during the night for refuelling.

After breakfast at 7.a.m. we board our coaches by 8.am.to drive to Yaroslav where we are welcomed by a jazz band before our city tour showing that they are very proud of their flowers and gardens. We also see the Church of the Epiphany of red brick with handcrafted tiles on a green roof and blue cupolas. Then we visited the Church of Elijah the Prophet, passing a tiny Church, exquisitely restored with fountains. and inside there were splendid frescoes and two wooden thrones, one for the Prophet and on for the Tsar. A change f tone is to visit the theatre, a small puppet theatre seating 300 and a children's theatre for 6000.

At this point we offer a comment about the guide accompanying us. She is a blonde lady called Laura, who teaches ancient history at the university, earning the equivalent of $ 60 a month (with no pay in July and August). Her outgoings are $20 for rent, $20 for her daughter at music school and $20 for everything else. Her father lived with her but had no pension. Shortage of money by individuals we met was a common grumble, so many of them assumed that "rich" western tourists would be willing to tip them. Travelling with us as a lecturer was Dr Zoya Zarubina,who had acted as Stalin's interpreter at the1945 Yalta conference between Churchill, Roosevelt and Stalin to discuss the settlement in Europe as World War 2 was drawing to a close. She was obviously a woman of some stature, but she was till included in the cruise director's guidance on tipping at the end of the cruise.

The next day was sunny and "warmish", so we sat on deck and watched Russia go by, including a barge trailing a raft of logs on the way to a timber yard until we arrived at Goritsky, a super genuine village with special carved wooden bus stops. The White Lake monastery was only partly restored as the money ran out.

We were back on board for a late lunch of kebabs and pancakes with caviar! Then we baked or slept in the sun until it was time for dinner, followed by listening to the world news.

Next morning after breakfast we arrive at Svirstroy as the cruise director and a guide conduct a question and answer session, taking any questions on contemporary Russia and it' s people, which was very interesting, and by the time the session had finished, local traders had arrived with various stalls set out along the pier. there were some very good quality items made by local craftsmen who were selling them. Some people were tempted, but we resisted, and we all went in for lunch and then enjoyed the sunshine as we set sail once more, soon followed by a "raft" of logs being towed by a barge on the way to timber yards.

Dinner that evening was rather special as it was our farewell dinner,(although there would be one more the following evening). The menu was: salad, peppers, hard boiled eggs, caviar, tomatoes, fish, cheese balls, ramekins of mushroom and cheese, chicken kiev, potatoes and, of course, tinned peas with pickled gherkin, cake, ice cream and coffee, together with Vodka, white wine and champagne. It soon became a very noisy dining room, with lots of photography and use of video cameras in use. We eventually went to bed, knowing that we would wake up in Saint Petersburg.

On our last full day the ship manoeuvred into an incredibly narrow berth so that passengers were able promptly to load the busses for the city tour.,starting in an industrial area and then along to the River Niva (invariably pronounced as "Reeva Neeva" by the guides) to a large number of naval vessels assembled as a celebration of 300 years of the Russian Navy. We crossed the French bridge and passed the Mint, which works 24 hours a day producing roubles. From here we moved to the Peter and Paul Fortress and the Cathedral with a fabulous pulpit and large tombs for previous Czars. Outside was a large bronze equestrian statue of Peter the Great set on a large granite base, around which newly married couples gathered for photographs with their families, and brides tossed their bouquets back over their heads with unmarried girls thought that they would soon be married if they caught the bouquet..Then it was back to the ship for lunch.

Refreshed after a good meal we returned to our coaches for our visit to The Winter Palace or Hermitage

The buildings were quite magnificent and the decorations of the individual rooms simply breath - taking. here were scores ad scores if paintings by, as examples, Leonardo da Vinci, Van Dyke, Rubens,, numerous Impressionists, as well as one room devoted to Matisse. Finally there was an unfinished sculpture with the odd title of "Young boy crouching".

Then it was back to the ship once more, for a quick snack before going ioff again, this time to the Maryinsky ballet at the theatre in the Hermitage with a performance of Giselle, which was delightful and included champagne in the interval. The place was packed with a highly appreciative audience, mainly of tourists. We were back on the ship in time for dinner at 10.15

Next day was definitely our last day, but not an early dash to the airport but a bit more culture before lunch and then to the airport for a 3.00.p.m flight to Vienna, starting with a short drive to the Peterhof, another magnificent building. It was built by the czars on the banks of the Gulf of Finland as a summer residence. The Grand Cascade with 143 fountains with gold statues. extravagance and imperial grandeur unparalleled! Then back to the ship for lunch of salad, fish, fishcakes, deep fried chicken, soup and ice cream before boarding the coaches for the last time, to arrive at the airport to catch the flight to Vienna, where we arrived in good time to take the on going flight to Heathrow and the shuttle to Manchester and the end of a memorable, interesting visit.

Chapter 9
The Bahamas: A rush for better seats

We had been on a cruise starting with sailing along the Panama canal from the Pacific to the Atlantic. From there we made our way up the coastal territories as far as Costa Rica with excursions into the rain forest canopy and then to Key West, the southernmost point of the USA, where we went ashore just for a morning after a brief scrutiny of our passports by an immigration officer, who posed a single question: "Any communicable disease?" Having reassured him on this point, we passed through, setting foot for the first (and so far only) time to enjoy a brief tour of the sights, principally the modest property which President Truman spent weekends at "The southern White house". and where Ernest Hemingway wrote "A Farewell to Arms". Then it was back on board for lunch and we were on our way to Grand Bahama

At this point we need to provide some background information. We were travelling on a ship called "Minerva" as we had a number of times before, which was chartered by Swan Hellenic, who chartered various airlines to convey a shipload of passengers out to the starting point of the cruise and back again from the final destination. We had not long finished our lunch when there was a public address announcement to tell us that the airline which had brought us out had since gone bust. An alternative had now been found that could take most people back from Grand Bahama as planned. An alternative British Airways flight could take other passengers 24 hours later, with those passengers remaining for that time in a luxury hotel with all expenses paid, and would be up-graded on the flight. Those wishing to take that offer should report to the office this afternoon.

Barbara went at once and was able to change our business class seats to first, but she was still not first in the queue! David Aaronawich, a columnist on *The Times,* was travelling on the cruise and subsequently wrote in his column about how tough the mainly elderly passengers were, with two examples, first was overheard when a woman said, "My sister has broken her arm, so I would like to change our excursion in Costa Rica from the full day to the half day, please." Secondly, his reaction to the public address announcement, "Suddenly there was a rush of pounding feet; sticks were cast aside and a breathless queue was quickly formed."

The hotel was suitably luxurious with our bedroom having two double beds and splendid en suite facilities. It was also patronised by Americans. On one of our early journeys in the lift, Derek showed his naievety by asking Barbara, "What was that woman doing walking up and down on the landing? She seemed to be in her underwear." Whereupon a gruff American as we got off the lift said, "Well she sure wasn't Little Red Riding Hood".

We enjoyed the whole of our time in Central America and the comfort of a first class bed with British Airways

Chapter 10

The Maldives: An endangered tropical paradise

We were on a cruise travelling from Mumbai to Colombo in 2017 when we had a stopover at Male, capital of The Maldives, a scattering of exquisite tropical islands in the Indian ocean, with waving palms, glittering white coral sands and translucent blue green seas that attracts holiday makers from many countries. (our younger daughter came here for her honey moon a year after our visit. It is a republic with no direct taxation, no political parties and virtually no crime. However, the idyll was badly affected by the 2004 tsunami that swept across this part the world. Some of the islands were totally destroyed and what remains is vulnerable to the effect of climate change.

For our visit the ship was anchored off shore, with a tender to take passengers to and from Male if they wished. We decided to go across and have a stroll along the sea front where we passed a fountain and a modern monument marking the establishment of the Republic of Male in 1968, following centuries of various sultanates, some benign, some corrupt. Moving to the history museum, it held a microcosm of years gone by. There were huge carved chairs lined with velvet alongside tiny carriages, apparently for the same monarch! clothes were in velvet and brocade, heavy with embroidery. Old photographs showed the sultans and their wives wearing these costumes. Elsewhere were artefacts from an ancient Buddhist monastery dated from before the sixth century and the conversion of the islands to Islam.

We returned to take the tender back to the shipfor some relaxation in the sun and looking forward to tomorrow and the highlight of our visit, lunch on an uninhabited tropical island.

The ship had re-located during the night and by 6.a.m. the ship was awake and most of the crew had "invaded" the island with lots of kit to get things ready and to clean the toilets. After breakfast we passengers followed them by tender. It was everybody's idea of a tropical island, with white sand, palm trees edging the warm sea, fantastic fish, including starfish seen even without a snorkel.

We found a spot in the shade of some palm trees and were quite settled, with the occasional little swim or walk until some of the crew came round with hot towels, followed by a tray with soft drinks and fruit punch. An amazing lunch followed. It was set out under awnings, massive barbecues were going with steaks, chicken, kebabs, burgers and grilled vegetables, accompanied by salads, jacket potatoes and breads. For dessert, a variety of cakes and fruit; all washed down by copious amounts of beer, wine, punch and soft drinks.

All day all manner of games were played; cricket, rounders, volley ball and finally a tug of war.

As we walked back to the tender to return to the ship, we

agreed that we had had a super day, on a holiday to remember!

Chapter 11

Flowers of the Aegean: A cruise aboard Minerva

At last time for the much looked forward to trip had arrived. We were anticipating warm sunshine in idyllic Greek islands and a return to some familiar Turkish seaside.

So we left for Gatwick; after passing through passport control and the security check (where Derek was frisked and had to remove his shoes) and walking to the departure lounge Barbara's mobile phone went off. It was from Gregory (!) asking where she was. After telling him, he was surprised she was still in the airport. "Where are you travelling to?" Her answer was "Why?" It turned out that her case was in the baggage area without a tag. How did they know it was hers? It had a card on the inside of the pocket with, luckily, the mobile number on; however that pocket had been padlocked shut!

We were a bit worried by this and went to the BA desk who were equally worried and clueless as to what was happening. Eventually it turned out that Gregory was a member of Global Baggage Solutions; a manager from the group came to explain the situation to her. But how was the case opened? Apparently easily with their skeleton keys.

After that excitement the flight was uneventful. The

monorail transfer between north and south terminals was as usual and we went to find which desk we had to go to tomorrow; this turned out to be in area D and it was already all set up for Swan Hellenic passengers.

We had already decided we weren't going to have dinner in the hotel so we got some good stuff from the 24hour M&S, returned to our room, ate and retired to bed ready for an early start the next morning.

The alarm went off at 5.45 to allow us to check in at 6.15, which we did without difficulty though there were plenty of others doing the same. We got ticked off because we hadn't brought our hand baggage to be checked for size; we had to do so when we returned to the terminal.

We had a good breakfast at the hotel and were eventually charged for just one as the dining room were so long sending the details up! We made the long trail back into the airport, purchased the paper and then were able to make our way to the boarding gate and were soon into our comfortable seats. The flight, with Thomas Cook, was uneventful, the food reasonable and the wine welcome.

Once at Athens airport and through passport control, we were guided onto waiting coaches for the hour long drive to Piraeus and Minerva. Our cabin was excellent, especially as we had a bottle of bubbly and a filled fridge.

Then the relentless familiar routine began; waiting anxiously for the cases to arrive at the cabin; ship's lifeboat drill, complete with life jackets and the disembodied voice of the captain; unpacking; the cruise in prospect and the assessment of the lecturers; dinner in the veranda café and finally and thankfully to bed.

Next day we had arrived in Piraeous and the first excursion was to the Parthenon and our guide was Lily, who was taking us round the new Acropolis museum. The journey from Piraeus initially took us across the peninsula passing the yacht harbour, full of a lot of expensive boats, and then the rather different traditional fishing harbour. After that we picked up the highway driving past stadia that years ago were just being built for the 2004 Olympics; there was the small volley ball stadium, the 'spiky' football one and the big sweeping main stadium.

The museum was spectacular and was based on the dimensions of the Acropolis itself. A gentle winding path took us to the entrance, through the security and the turnstile to the first gallery. In the first case there were beautiful water jars with three handles; two at the side for carrying and one at the back for pouring and used to carry the water for ritual bathing. They were decorated telling the role of women. One had a bride on it represented as a nymph because that would bring not only fertility into the family but also life and vitality. Other illustrations showed crafts such as spinning, weaving and Aphrodite, goddess of marriage.

Up the flight of stairs and past a huge sculpture of two lions tearing each other apart, really gruesome! On the same floor were fine marble statues of male and female figures; the females all young and beautiful with belted, draped dresses and long hair; the young males without beards, naked, powerfully built with one leg forward. All the features were designed to symbolise "the new citizen".

Older men were all bearded, because tradition demanded they never shaved; they were dressed in a coat like garment and were often with a sacrificial bull or with a horse, because horsemen were always of high rank. The statues were idealised people not portraits.

The upper storey had the marbles of the frieze of the Parthenon exactly as the original but at eye level so they can be seen easily. Some of the pieces were originals, some were good plaster copies. There were some gaps, clearly labelled "Originals in the British Museum" or "Seized by the BM". The frieze, like the original, is in two halves, meeting in the middle and is of a procession of proud horsemen; chariots; men with large shields indicating their aristocratic roots; athletes; acrobats jumping on and off moving chariots (reminiscent of the bull leaping of Knossos).

Then there were the old men, the musicians and teenagers, all in groups, representing the classes of the pedagogues in the gymnasium and finally the women with the ritual vases for bathing. All of this was watched over by the seated gods. It was both interesting and informative. We had free time to look again at the exhibits, to go outside to a spectacular open courtyard and café from where we could see the Acropolis and area around it. Then came the difficult bit of finding our way out! We kept coming upon 'swans' wandering rather anxiously and wondering if they would ever emerge or be kept hostage until the Elgin marbles were restored! We did, of course, find the exit and the coach and returned in time to have lunch outside, just before sailing. Then it was off towards the Corinth Canal. As we left the shelter of the harbour the wind got up and the temperature went down.

As we approached the eastern entrance to the canal the pilot boat brought the three pilots who were needed to navigate us through, not the same ones that we'd had on Spirit. Then the tug arrived to guide, not pull, us the 6km length of the canal. It was really cold all the way through with the head wind blowing against us. We also had such a strong current against us that the ship's engines were working at a rate that would normally have allowed it to sail along at 11 knots but in fact we could only do 2 knots!

As well as the crowds on one of the road bridges waving us on our way, we also saw an agile lesser kestrel as it swooped along the sheer sides. Almost as agile was the fine red fox that ran up and down the right-hand bank. At one of the narrowest points Minerva actually "kissed" a bank, there was no damage except to the captain's pride. So two hours later and after a glass of ouzo, we emerged successfully at the west end under the super suspension bridge now connecting the Peloponnese and the main land. In the 6th century BC the Corinthians designed a sort of railway across the isthmus at this its narrowest point to avoid the dangerous 322km sail round the Peloponnese. Ships were loaded onto carts and then dragged across the isthmus on a smooth paved road. our traverse was certainly easier!

Next day our trip was to Katakolon. We set off for the castle in Chlemoutsi at 8.45 a.m. driving through the countryside; mountains in the middle and plains on the coast and rich agricultural land growing olives, raisins and acres of polytunnels growing vegetables and fruit including melons. We saw the first of many Judas trees, laden with brilliant purple blossom. They are so named because of the belief that Judas hung himself from one of these trees after betraying Jesus. The fields were full of red poppies and the houses covered in wisteria, the so called "Tears of the Virgin".

The castle is described as Frankish, founded in1220 to 1223 by the crusaders and very reminiscent of English castles, somebody had said it reminded them of Kenilworth, Even though it had been occupied by many invaders (Catalans, Turks and Venetians) it remained much as it was originally. The large outer enclosure was approached through a four walled tower with three arched gates, one adapted for chucking down hot oil and large stones onto the enemy. The walls obviously were extremely thick and had two other towers and were crenellated.

The inner enclosure was built on the highest part of the hill and it was where the residences of the important nobility of the castle were found. There was a well preserved room of a prince and his company; it had two storeys and a large fireplace. One of the other rooms had been developed as a charming little museum housing all sorts of artefacts; there were incredibly fine needles, coins, jewellery and ornaments crafted from stone and shells.

In spite of the many uneven steps in the castle we enjoyed the visit and the views from the walls. We made our way down the steep hill and passed houses with window boxes and pots full of geraniums, to the village of Kastro where several cafes tempted us. We settled on one with tables outside and not overrun by swans; there was one couple already sitting with their drinks, they were John, who was *very* tall, and his wife,

Joan who wasn't! A really nice couple from Australia. It turned out that there were quite a few Aussies as well as New Zealand passengers on board, unusual in our experience on previous cruises on Minerva.

Derek went in to get his soft drink and coffee for Barbara, who sat in the sun trying to see why her camera had frozen. It turned out to be faulty batteries thank goodness. She thought it had died. Derek seemed to be a long time but eventually emerged. He had had some difficulty ordering Barbara's coffee; his drink could be pointed out in the fridge, so he waited patiently at the bar. She meanwhile had enjoyed an excellent coffee and a glass of cold water which had been brought out to her.

It was soon time to move on, so we got back into the coach which had to do a tricky U-turn; suddenly there was a very loud crunching noise; we thought at the very least we'd demolished a motor bike, but no, apparently it was 'just' the undercarriage of the coach attacking the kerb! As we drove to the Byzantine church we passed a number of roadside stalls and lorries selling fruit and vegetables. They were from local farms which were run by gypsies who came originally from India but who are now settled, no longer nomadic, and are well integrated into their communities but retaining their own lifestyle. They attracted attention by the use of very loud loudhailers!

The ruined church we had stopped to see certainly was a ruin set in the middle of a small town. There were gothic arches but little else of interest. We arrived back at the ship for a late lunch and to watch as we left Katakolon. The afternoon was taken up by lectures: Cycladic art by Lesley Fitton, birds by Tim

Earl and Philip Cribb on flowers, followed by afternoon tea. Our appetites had been wetted for the cruise ahead of us. Then it was time to glam up for the welcome party and gala dinner.

The reception was fine, plenty of fizz and an announcement by Paul of the engagement of one of the swan staff to the Captain! We ate in the Veranda with Saida and Clare, a pleasant couple who we dined with several times during the cruise. There were two of the strange coincidences that one often comes across; Saida's late husband and his father and grandfather both went to MGS. where Derek went. She had some photos from early in the 20th century and had wanted to contact the school's archivist, and now she could through Derek. She was a good companion, an English graduate, and happy to try to track down Derek's quotation about the" banks of Asphodel" (she never managed to). Later she became a bit tetchy saying that Clare was cross with her so she was keeping her distance!

Clare, a little older than Saida, also an English graduate and very cultured; the coincidence with her was that she knew and had been a fellow student with, Jean Huntington, who was a member of our church at home. We dined and fed well in good company!

Next day we were in Kalamata.

We had a leisurely morning and a late breakfast with Derek and Sheila from Scotland; much younger than us but we were to spend a lot of time with them over the next two weeks. He was quiet and worked for the Ordinance Survey; she was a teacher trainer and "alternative" with a punk-style hair-do in black, red and purple (not what one usually expects on Minerva). We were joined by an elderly widow, Joan; elderly in years but not attitude, and completely dizzy!

We set off walking along the front past the fishing boats and fishermen, and their wives, mending the nets and doing a roaring trade in the morning's catch. We struck away from the sea too soon so we missed the good scarf shop (it was becoming apparent that warm clothes and accessories would be at a premium) and the spectacular church. The streets we saw were undistinguished; poor housing and uninteresting shops though there were several displaying expensive and beautiful wedding fripperies and chocolatiers with fabulous Easter eggs and baskets; this seemed at odds with the rest of the shops. One intriguing feature was a pretty little church set, at an angle, right across a road. Which came first – the church or the road?

After lunch we were on a scenic tour of Mani, the southern part of the Peloponnese; an isolated, mainly agricultural, community between mountain and sea. Visible from most of the area was the snow-capped Mount Taygetus and on its steep slopes Greek pines, Black pine and on lower slopes Spanish broom, Mimosa (Acacia), olives and Eucalyptus. The fields were separated by dry stone walls, built because so much stone had to be cleared from the land to make it possible to farm. We asked about the "smoking" olive trees. it was an old method of pest control, apparently. nearly all the houses we passed had small towers on the side and were, thus, tower houses. This tradition dates back to the 13th century when there was a strong clan system in this part of Greece. The most powerful family had the biggest property in the centre of the settlement with a fort like house; the lower families had smaller houses. Each clan had its own laws and protected their territory fiercely.

Gradually we descended to the coast passing on the way a profusion of wild flowers. In the fields and gardens were beehives, many of them in bright colours; regional honey is a great delicacy. We stopped in the village Areopoli; it was extremely cold and windy and the village was very much closed up, few shops open and only one small church to peep into and another one, built of stone with a fine stone bell tower. We were *so* cold that everyone made for one of the two cafes and ordered hot drinks; we had strong coffee It also had a clean toilet even though it was "outside".

In the right weather it would have been pleasant to wander round but not today. The return drive was nice and we arrived back in before the last embarkation and said farewell to Kalamata without too many regrets.

When we woke up we found we were already at anchor in the bay of Monemvasia. The weather wasn't kind to us; it was pouring with rain and with a very strong wind blowing. Nevertheless we ventured onto the deck and were admiring the white typically Greek town across the bay and thinking it would be ok but not that special. The ship then swung on its anchor to reveal the most spectacular fortified town that climbed from the sea up the hill to the citadel at the top, all surrounded by impressive walls.

The colony dates from the middle ages when it was fortified, cut off from the mainland and connected only by a bridge of 14 arches. It was besieged for three years in 1248 and eventually captured by William de Villehardouin. He restored it and held it for 25 years but then had to surrender it to the Byzantines. From the 15th century it passed to the Pope, the Venetians and the Turks. Today the surviving structures are Venetian from the 16th century. It looked delightful – but we were to observe it only from the sea, we were unable to launch the tenders and in any case the port authorities refused to open the landing facility as it was deemed too dangerous.

Unwillingly we had to agree because we watched difficulties experienced by the boat's tender, which had been sent across to the landing point to bring the port police to Minerva to discuss the situation and, of course they had to be taken back. They struggled against a strong current and gale force winds. On the outward run one of the sailors had lost his safety helmet and was in real danger of going off the narrow ledge to which he was clinging. Somehow one of the strengthened windows in the tender had been broken, an indication of the conditions. It took the tender crew several attempts to get into the side of Minerva and connect the straps to the winches so they could be winched up into position. When they succeeded those of us left watching, clinging onto the handrail having removed glasses which were in great danger of being lost, were mightily relieved. The Captain then closed and locked all doors to the outer decks as it was so dangerous.

He attempted to get into another port, again without success so we set off for Aghios Nikolaos. The amazing thing was that in spite of the heavy seas and the wind there wasn't too much movement on board, because of his clever sailing into the head wind whenever possible. The only difficulty proved to be carrying ones soup to ones place in the veranda.

The rather longer day at sea was filled with two more good lectures and afternoon tea!

The weather allowed us to berth so we could go on our morning tour to Malia. The area on Crete was new to us and we were looking forward to seeing the countryside. We hadn't realised that during the time Crete was occupied by the Ottoman Turks no church bells could be rung and schools had to be conducted in secret. Although we didn't see them this time, older men can still be seen in traditional costume, bearded and with a splendid moustache.

The first stop was at Malia's Minoan palace; it had been built in two phases, the first and second palace periods. The remains are extensive, though much damaged by earthquakes, so they really are piles of stones! The lay out was easy to picture within the existing walls and with remaining stairs leading up to platforms on which kings and princes would have sat There were several bases of pillars which indicated the extent of arenas and colonnades. An area under cover to protect archaeologists and visitors from the heat of the sun was still being excavated. Here we could see the cellars where oil had been stored in massive stone jars on each side of a central gangway which sloped gently down to a funnelled drain which removed spilt oil.

The site itself was in a delightful situation, surrounded by mountains and full of wild flowers. This meant lots of the swans were busy taking photographs, not of the ruins but of the flowers, so much so it caused Derek to comment on the varying priorities of our party: flowers or a significant site of antiquity, several thousand years old. It was clear where *his* priority lay.

*   *   *

From here we zig zagged up the winding road to the convent of Panghia Kera Kardiotissa, through a little village with its fruit and vegetables displayed on the pavement; sacks of potatoes and huge bunches of bananas which we had seen growing in vast poly tunnels as we drove up. Most of the houses were built in limestone and marble, only the luxury ones also had wood.

The convent was set in beautiful surroundings, high in the mountains with fabulous views; it houses 200 nuns today, dedicated to healing as well as spreading the gospel. They were a reclusive order and hid away from the tourists though we glimpsed one or two of them. The church was a splendid example of a Byzantine church. A church had been on the site since the 11th century, the present building dated from the 13 and 14th centuries. It was, unusually, three naved and had an extension at the east end. Its most famous piece was the icon of the Virgin in chains, a very beautiful icon with an interesting history. The icon, which was associated with miracles, was stolen and taken to Heraklion; when it was found it was carried back, all the way on foot and chained to one of the pilgrims. When it arrived back at the convent it was again chained, to a pillar, which still exists. The icon is now in the church incorporated in the iconostasis and beside it a chain that the faithful can still use when praying.

On the opposite side of the iconostasis is Christ represented, bizarrely, as an orthodox bishop! The iconostasis was beautifully carved and incorporated small but exquisite icons of St. Peter and Paul; Adam and Eve in the Garden of Eden and then after they'd been expelled. At the back of the church were some important frescoes, but in a poor state. Other icons were of St. Anne, its patron saint, and of St. Anthony. Also a charming painting of 'the tender Virgin'.

In the courtyard there was the pillar to which the icon had been chained, a small altar blackened by smoke from candles and a large stone table on which is placed communion bread for sharing at the big festivals of the orthodox calendar (only the priests have wine). It had been a delightful visit, one of the best in the cruise I think, and to cap it all the toilets were immaculate!

The last part of the drive was up to a viewpoint over the Lasithi Plain; a fertile high plateau, 2760 feet above sea level and one of the highest inhabited areas in the Mediterranean, with a population of about 3000. The view was certainly spectacular stretching for miles both north and south and in its grounds some windmills once used for irrigation of the plain. Naturally there was a shop and café dominating the point, welcome on several counts not least for the purchase of a warm scarf. We were back at the ship for lunch and Barbara was then ready to go again by 1.30 p.m.

The drive retraced the journey we had done this morning (so much so that Derek decided to stroll round Aghios Nikolas instead but we had lots of stops for flowers! At these stops the keen swans leapt out with flower reference books, keen not to miss a word from Philip or a single specimen!

The first stop was at the side of a very busy road so there were dire warnings of the danger of going for that special specimen across the road! There were lovely flowers even orchids in such an inauspicious place. One gentleman, though, took a real tumble over a hidden cable getting a cut face and broken glasses – such are the perils of botanising!

The list of flowers we saw was impressive and too long for here. As well as flowers we had Tim with us to spot, at a great distance some of the birds like yellow leg gull (we didn't even see it) and a raven (which we did), kestrels and hooded crows. At a stop later some of us abandoned the flowers in favour of birds but they were keeping a low profile except for the grey heron.

The Lasithi plateau was interesting as we drove through it; a vast plain once flooded and now drained, divided into squares separated by canals and with many "windmills", now water pumps, which are used for irrigation of the land. There were lots of apple trees and other fruit trees, an important resource in the area as well as potatoes. In the winter the fields are full of barley or artichokes.

We were extremely late back due to our many stops especially the last one to photograph the irises! Actually it was a nice stop in woodland with gentle slopes and 'ordinary' flowers, which were lovely.

The weather forecast wasn't good so there were two plans for tomorrow; Plan A was to sail for Delos and Syros (Tinos had already been cancelled, the port was closed because of the sea conditions). Plan B was for Mykonos and Syros; we would see!

It was obvious that housekeeping was expecting the worse. The wardrobes had been secured with specially made locks; all the bottles, glasses and the ice bucket had been moved to the floor. It was a bumpy night and in spite of all the precautions Barbara's water glass flew off the bedside unit showering her in the process.

In the morning the decision was made:it was to be Mykonos. Even though we had been before, in similar circumstances 10 years ago, we still enjoyed the wander round the tiny, twisting alleys of white cube-shaped houses. It was built like that to defy the wind and pirate raids but today it was losing the battle against a really bitter wind, blowing hard round all the corners.. We had a much needed cup of coffee that cost a ridiculous number of euros, and were pleased to find the island's mascot, a pelican, was still there in the main square. His name was Petros and supposed to be a direct descendent of the original one. Minerva was berthed at the *new* cruise terminal which meant we had to have a shuttle bus taking us to town and back again. That explained why we had remembered walking straight in last visit.

We were glad to be back for lunch; it was a Greek-themed barbeque, so we braved the wind outside and had an interesting lunch, anchoring down the salad before the wind blew it away. We sailed off to Syros at 3pm and Chris Kelly lectured to some of us before afternoon tea, when there was a lot of comfort eating!

Minerva berthed right near to town so we could set off at 6pm for an orientation walk. The Greek guides really earned their keep; they had to prepare for Delos and Tinos, they were cancelled so it was off to Mykonos and remembering facts about that; then more preparation for Syros, not a very popular destination though it is getting more tourists. It is the commercial and administrative centre of the Cyclades.

Ermoupoli is the main town and leading port of the island, set in a safe, large harbour, the reason we had headed for it. It was very busy all evening with ferry boats coming and going. We walked from the ship, through the port car park and into the pedestrianised area, the Marble road, genuinely made of marble imported from Tinos. It led to the main square, also paved with marble, and lined by palms and cafes, most of them closed. Dominating the square was the large neo-classical town hall and a bandstand, all in marble!

All the elegant lights round the square were swathed in purple and white material and flags flying purple, all apparently for Holy Week. What was not so 'Holy' was the massive example of road rage on the street corner between an elderly moped rider and a young sports car driver. It involved a lot of shouting and raised fists. The guide declined to interpret the language so we never knew what it was about though we speculated that the moped driver had, unknowingly, cut up the young man.

We had dinner in a deserted veranda before walking back into town. Many shops were now open and couples and families were wandering along the streets. Many of the shops were showing Easter candles, decorated eggs and 'hens'. Apparently hard boiled eggs would be painted on Thursday ready for midnight on Easter Day when they would be eaten. We walked back along the quayside lined by bars, some busy and others empty.We didn't have to be back on board till 23.45 but we didn't find anything else to keep us in town, so it was back to the ship, hot drinks and bed.

*   *   *

Next day we started at sea. That means at least two things; we don't have to get up too early; there are lectures to go to. Both of us took advantage of the first and one of us went to "Greece and Turkey: Ataturk and Venizalos" and both, after coffee, to "Inside Greek Churches", with a lot about icons, which was excellent.

Amazingly we emerged to warm sunshine!. We couldn't believe it after the last few days… It was a lovely sail, with land on both sides; Asia Minor on the port side and Greek Dodecanese islands starboard. We were able to eat out in comfort and watch as Symi came into view. It was more like an Italian town than a Greek Island. Classical style houses in creams, browns and occasionally pale blue, all with white outlines and pediments. They all had small shuttered windows to protect from the cold in winter and extreme heat in summer. The walls were, apparently, of stone, under the paint, and at least 60cm thick, also to protect from the elements.

The island is rocky and barren but thrived on its sponge-diving fleet and boat building, once launching 500 boats a year. In the 17th century it was one of the richest islands of the area. But with the arrival of artificial sponges and steam power and then occupation by the Italians its good fortune collapsed and with it the population, from 23,000 to 6,000 by WWII. The main income now comes from tourism. It is without a natural source of water so all of it has to come from desalination and then be pumped up to the houses and hotels.

On the western side of the harbour is the clock tower, from1800s in blue and white Italianate style. Next to it was an amazing police station; three storeys in brilliant white and a red roof. The upper floors were arcaded with blue windows and doors and the top of the third storey crenellated in a most elaborate way. As different a police station as you could imagine. The harbour is a busy, thriving fishing and ferry port. The colourful fishing boats line the harbour promenade. A little further round were impressive yachts, several registered in the UK.

The town of Symi is divided into two parts; the lower part, Gialos with theharbour and its houses,, and the upper, older part, Chorio, where most of the churches are and which involves climbing 375 steep steps; we didn't!

Two hills dominate the skyline; one has the remains of a Frankish castle and windmills; the other once had the Acropolis but now a forest of mobile phone satellite dishes!

We walked through the car park and over an ancient bridge with shoals of fish swimming below and along the narrow quayside road, dodging the many, noisy mopeds. Many of the shops were selling sponges, all claiming to be genuine and from the local sponge divers, though according to the guides they are in fact artificial.

There were souvenir shops, cafes and restaurants. Having got as far as we could one way we turned around and went back the other way, past Minerva which as it was berthed right on the quay side completely dominated the place. It brought out the locals to see this unusual sight. Meanwhile our walk took us round the corner and to a delightful café right on the beach, indeed part of it jutting out into the sea; unfortunately it was closed.

We seem to have explored all that Symi had to offer so it was back for dinner followed by a gentle constitutional along the quay.

Next day we were in the island of Rhodes. This meant a lovely, lazy morning in the sun for Barbara, while Derek dutifully attended several lectures. then an excellent Filipino-themed lunch during which we sailed into Rhodes which was delightful.

We were going different ways this afternoon; Babara was off to the interior of the island and the slopes of Mt. Profitas Illias. Derek was doing the Rhodes town walk to remember and admire the old city. Barbara,s botany trip was so popular that they agreed to take two coaches, instead of one, and for Philip, Tim and Marian (Philip's knowledgeable wife) to spread themselves between the two groups. It worked extremely well.

We left at 1.30 with a run through the outskirts of Rhodes where our Greek guide gave us a short lecture about the island. The total population is 120,000, half of them in Rhodes town though in 468BC it was ten times that size! We passed a huge modern "multicultural" cemetery, in other words Jews, Christians both Catholic and protestant are buried in the same area. Opposite was an even bigger site of the ancient necropolis.

A little farther along was the farmers' market, we had hoped to walk there later but it was much too far. Outside the market there was a strange mixture of things that would be important for the Easter celebrations. There were rows of wreaths; these would be laid during the long church services of Good Friday and Easter day, between long readings of the bible, and acting out of the Crucifixion. Then there were bags and bags of BBQ coals; every family have a celebratory barbeque at the end of the service on Sunday.

Our first stop was on a very busy roadside, with strict instructions (again) not to cross the road whatever we saw on the other side! There was plenty on our verge including orchids and asphodels and a lovely clouded yellow butterfly but no birds to Tim's disappointment.

Along the coast we past a Miami-style development but we left it behind and began to climb up through the pine forests; as well as pines there were ornamental ash or the Persian lilac, Washintonia (a fan leaved conifer) and Allepo pines. In among the trees were beautiful flowers; cyclamen, crown marigolds and of course orchids – everywhere - spotted by the eagle eyes of Philip.

Our next stop was deep in the woods and at a charming little white Byzantine church with frescoes inside. Around the church were all manner of flowers, including … orchids! and blue anemones, cyclamen and bee orchids but perhaps most intriguing several specimens of a bright red parasitic plant. In the gardens of the church were a number of peacocks, one even displayed his tail for us.

Back onto the coaches and further in to the pine forest where we stopped at the Elafos hotel; a delightful building reminiscent of the properties in the Cameron Highlands. They had arranged cold drinks for us, very welcome. There's always the awkward one – a man who demanded a *hot* drink, he didn't get one. Later in the holiday he was heard asking for a cold drink when hot were on offer!

Walking through the woods was lovely and there were

lots of flowers, though again few birds. Some of the familiar ones were vetches, peonies, cyclamen, asphodels and a type of buttercup. Some of the more unusual plants were a mandrake (the one which screams when pulled up!); Jack in the Pulpit and various orchids that we all duly knelt on the ground to use our macro lens to photograph them (not to pay homage to!). Up one of the tracks we found a deserted house which we decided could be developed into a jolly nice home.

We moved down the mountain to the coastal plain past peach orchards and then small developments of holiday homes with various shops serving them; fields of crown marigolds and bright red poppies and flower shops. But nearer to Rhodes there were massive groups of monstrous hotels/resorts.

It had been a good trip, pleasant company, lovely flowers and newly acquired knowledge. After dinner we decided we would both go into the old city and see what it was like In the evening so we went into dinner early and then set off quickly, on a rather wet dull evening. Darkness fell quickly; it was spooky in the dark alleys as the cats slunk furtively by. There were few restaurants open and virtually no lights, this made it difficult to find our way. After enquiring the way several times we eventually found our way back to the gate from the city and made our way along the quay to the ship where we were told we were the last passengers to return!

We sailed during the night and left Greek waters; by the time we awoke we were in Turkish waters. Barbara woke up early and went to get cups of tea and then to join Tim bird watching (there weren't any!). By breakfast time we were in Fethiye. It is supposed to date back to the Trojan wars and stands today on the ruins of the ancient city if Telmessos. Earthquakes in 1856 and 1957 levelled nearly all the edifices that were standing and today it is a modern little town rising up from the harbour onto the mountain side. Minerva had been expected to anchor off the town but for some reason was able to berth, which wasmuch more convenient!

We had booked to go on one of the tours but decided against it in favour of just wandering. That meant we could have a leisurely start, so leisurely in fact that we decided to watch the gullet trips set off. This proved most entertaining. We saw Derek and Sheila board the boat and settle themselves and their picnic (which was, apparently, disappointing, especially when left in the sun), right at the front unlike the rest of the group who sat sedately inside under the canopy. The second group duly walked along the quay and onto their, rather less nice, boat and it was time to be waved off by the watchers on deck.

Then the fun started! The second boat manoeuvred from its berth and set off. The first and rather larger boat then attempted to leave but had no room at all and got completely stuck in spite of a member of its crew lying full length attempting to push it away from the somewhat larger Minerva. The extremely close proximity to Minerva's bow caused no fewer than four officers to rush out to the bridge. In the end the other gullet had to return, attach a rope and pull it away from the quay so it could do a 10-point turn and sail away. At this point we realised the captain and his fiancée were on the "rescue" gullet and finding it rather amusing, certainly unconcerned!

After the excitement we walked along the harbour and into the "bazaar" – not a memorable one. There was the inevitable encounter that we, as usual, fell for. As we were strolling along a very pleasant young man approached us asking if we were English and if we would allow him to practise his English with us. We agreed (why are we so gullible?) and had a few minutes nice conversation but then came the inevitable "Please come and accept my hospitality." There was absolutely no refusing him and we ended up in the spice shop, on a stool or a chair retrieved from the back for Derek, drinking mint tea out of dubious glasses. Then followed "Where you from?" "You like football?" "I like football and basketball, but not cricket." Then came the hard sell of spices and Turkish delight. With some difficulty we refused to buy anything and eventually extricated ourselves and left. It did mean that on the way back we had to avoid that particular street.

After a pricey coke we wandered back to the harbour past the old Turkish baths, still used, and with towels hung on the line above the roof. We watched the fishing boats coming in and the old couple diligently mending the nets. Further along was a young man high up in the crow's nest of a tall sailing ship.

We were then able to sit in the sun; we even had to move after a short time, into the shade.

After lunch we set off to Kayakoy village; as ever the journey was lovely, initially through the town and on the outskirts we saw the blocks of tall posh flats, apparently a British community. We wondered if the purchasers had actually seen where they were situated – high above the town, on an unmade road with no public transport. In one of the villages was a man carrying a tray of bagels on his head and then along a tree-lined lane running by the side of a crystal-clear stream. So we arrived to the eerie deserted village.

It was once home to 2,500 Anatolian Greek Christians, who were repatriated to Greece after WWI, in 1923, as part of a population exchange agreement between the Greek and Turkish governments. The Turkish people didn't want to live there so it has been abandoned ever since. There are something like 500 cuboid houses in various states of ruin. They are separated by narrow lanes; clearly motor cars never reached this village. It was such a strange feeling wandering through the houses thinking of the people who lived and worked there. One of the most intact buildings was the lower church which had still got some of its frescoes and a black and white mosaic floor.

Some of the party clambered up the steep stony path towards the church at the top; several gave up at various stages as it became even steeper and more uneven or when vertigo finally took over. Some of the determined swans struggled on with sticks and even resorting to sliding on bottoms! The views from the top were spectacular, right across to the sea.

Down at the bottom of the hill refreshments were definitely called for and a café owner with an eye to the main chance had opened up and was selling very welcome cold drinks.come. Somewhat later than scheduled we set off back; one gentleman was reunited with his bag, once he found the right coach; another lady was spotted walking quickly along with another group just prior to getting on their coach, the fact they were German seemed to have escaped her notice!

So we left the strange place, a UNESCO world friendship and peace village, to go back to its sleep. Once again our tour group was late back but soon everything was set to go and the ship left for Bodrum.

After dinner the crew put on their excellent show with some really talented performers, including Andrew Galang who had a lovely voice, as did the housekeeper, Ann Bennet. Other members of the crew, mainly those from the Philippines, did their fabulous dances, familiar from previous cruises but none the worse for that; the coconut dance, the flower dance and the bamboo dance, with passenger "volunteers". The funniest item was the puppet song and dance, with the 'legs' of the puppets worked from behind by two of the crew.

I think we all agreed it was one of the best shows we'd seen.

We arrived at Bodrum duly set off to visit the castle, St. Peter's built by the Knights of St. John; a pleasant walk along the marina where we saw one of the many marching bands of children and teenagers. It was a public holiday and children's day; hence the activities and the crowds - they gave the place a great atmosphere.

The 15th/16thcentury-castle was great, with ramparts, watch towers, great crenellated walls and narrow walkways. It was along one of these we set off once through the impressive iron gates. We went first to the reconstruction of a 7th- century ship; it had been well done and gave a good idea of what life may have been like serving in the ship. Most intriguing were the dozens of amphora stacked in straw. Apparently their round shape, which seemed inconvenient for storage, was to better preserve the liquid contents. From the reconstruction we went out again into the sunshine and the gardens with the planted urns (or boxes as the guide said) and the peacocks, one of which actually displayed his tail. We walked up onto the ramparts of the castle to admire the views; in the distance, windmills across the harbour and the hill where the Turkish army have their holiday accommodation. The first tower we got to was the English one with the English lion proudly shown in relief. Inside there was typical furniture that would have been seen in the prince's time.

In the treasure house were some exquisite artefacts like the glass ingot, tiny "duck" boxes, carvings in ivory, lots of gold, an Egyptian scarab and the seal of Nefertiti (indicating trade with and the influence from Egypt), a beautiful two handed pilgrims flask as well as the more mundane fish hooks. Perhaps the most astounding thing was a 14th-century notebook; the writing surface of wax, the binding of wood and a place to put the stylus for writing on the wax. It was so like a modern notebook that we were all astounded.

Emerging from the castle we walked along the marina, up into town where we passed a huge decoration, like an upside down chandelier, in red and white hanging outside a restaurant,a very striking advertisement. The road took us to the Mausoleum of King Mausolus – "Something not to be missed" and "One of the wonders of the world." Well, it may once have been, but no more; there was nothing on the site but piles of stones, a few walls and the bases of columns. Very difficult to see the wonder of the world! However in the small museum was a super model of what the mausoleum would have looked like and it was magnificent. It would have stood on a colossal base on which were life size sculptures. On this a narrower base with more figures surmounted by ionic columns and they held up dozens of lions, horses and chariots. The pediment supported another huge four horse chariot. Perhaps in its time it was a wonder!

Walking back along the quay side, we passed more of the lively marching bands; children in school uniform and in traditional dress. It was delightful. We decided we needed a drink before going back to the bus for the transfer to the ship so we sat in a bar on the edge of the marina and enjoyed a Turkish beer.

We sailed at three and had a lovely relaxed afternoon either reading or listening to lectures. The day finished with a pleasant light music programme from the classical musicians, which we actually liked.

Next day we sailed into Kusadasi at 7 a.m. We had had a dilemma as to what to do today, but decided to go to Ephesus and it proved to be an excellent tour; we were glad we hadn't missed it. On the bus we were, inevitably, given all sorts of information, some interesting, some not and much subsequently forgotten. The use of the land *was* interesting; its fertility due to many springs and because it was reclaimed from the river as it began to silt up 3000 years ago creating its fertility. The fields are quite small because if divided more were available for the poorer people to cultivate. There were a lot of mulberry trees to feed the silk worms that, apparently, only feed on the female trees;

cotton is also grown so weaving, both silk and cotton, has been an important craft for a long time.

A fine new road took us to the ancient site of Ephesus which, according to legend, was founded by the Amazon women! It was inhabited from the Bronze Age but changed location several times, usually to be nearer to the sea or to escape malarial swamps.

From the point where the coach dropped us we walked along a shady path, and entered through the Harbour Gate and past the stadium, used for chariot racing, athletics and gladiatorial combats. Then by the church of the Virgin Mary; built by the Romans in 2nd century AD as a trading centre but converted to a church in the 4th century. Ephesus is, of course of some significance to Christians with its letter to the Ephesians from St. Paul. He is believed to have been in the city between 65 and 68 AD and may well have been imprisoned here. A silver smith, Demetrius, stirred up the people against St. Paul and when he preached in the theatre they stoned him. The crowd and Demetrius especially, objected to his preaching because they would lose a lot of trade and income if they couldn't make the silver images of the other gods.

The theatre is spectacular even though one third remains unexcavated. It sits on the hillside and could seat 25,000. It has lost much of its decoration but it is still quite an experience to sit on the stone seats and think how many bottoms have sat here previously. There were of course *crowds* of people wandering or being addressed by guides.

Then we walked along the Marble Way connecting the theatre with the Library of Celsus. There are a number of reliefs scratched in the stones of the road; one, a left foot which indicates, or confirms, the way to the brothel; another is a circle with 8 lines from one side to the other crossing in the middle, the form of the Maltese Cross, and representing the Greek letters IXOYZ i.e. Jesus, Christ, God, Son and Saviour. The Library is stunning and cleverly restored in the 20th century. There are eight columns, arranged in two stories; each of the columns is supported by lead plates at the top and bottom allowing a play of 50 centimetres to withstand earthquakes. There are two of the remaining statues standing between the white marble ionic columns. Steps lead into the large main room which is 16 by 10 metres. On the edge of the "road" are splendid pieces of marble that once decorated the library; the carvings on them were realistic – helmets, wreaths of leaves and flowers and heads of the emperor. Apparently there was a tunnel between the Library and a brothel across the road!

Looking across the site we could see a lot of plastic covering something; this proved to be recently discovered Roman Houses. They were open to the public but with a separate ticket, which we hadn't got, but they were well worth the visit apparently. They had been buried for so long they had retained much of the detail of their architecture and decoration.

We wandered back along the Marble Road past the Agora to look at the theatre again. From one of raised viewpoints we looked over the site and realised how huge it was. We didn't however explore further, we'd enjoyed what we'd seen and made our way back to the entrance, running by the souvenir sellers, though we did buy a book.

After lunch we took a nostalgic walk to Pigeon Island. It

was Sunday and it seemed like all the world and his wife were also walking to Pigeon Island. The island itself seemed rather tattier than we remembered and of the little café where we'd had a pleasant meal there was no sight. The only place to have a drink was an unappealing café/bar on the quay side, so we gave it a miss and wandered back to Minerva and afternoon tea. The rest of the afternoon and evening passed nicely and unremarkably.

Next we had a day at Sea. It was quite a relief to have a day off and not to be going on an excursion, we never thought we'd say that but it had been a hectic cruise and the days we had had at sea were unplanned and not therefore "thought into". It was a pleasant day in the usual routine when at sea on Minerva; lectures; coffee; more lectures then lunch, a BBQ today with a seafood theme, very good too though a bit windy, we had to hang onto our lettuce, again! Having given lectures a miss for the sun, in the morning I actually went to two lectures; one given by Philip on the flowers we'd seen during the cruise; this was followed by a London-Paris afternoon tea.

We were then in the Dardanelles and had a deck talk as we sailed through, a narrow strait connecting the Mediterranean with the Black sea or more precisely the Aegean and the sea of Marmara. It was a tricky sail for the captain because there are two opposing currents that flow all the time. One runs from the Sea of Marmara towards the Aegean and an undercurrent in the opposite direction. We passed close to Gallipoli on the European side and on the other side was Asia, we heard about the history as we went. On this shore we saw the massive grey stone Turkish war memorial at Canakkale and a little further on the low white tower indicating the Australian war cemetery.

In the evening we had the Captain's farewell party which meant more champagne and canapés and small talk with people, some of whom we had met before and others we hadn't! Mary-Jane had asked us to join them for the Gala dinner (Shelia and Derek were on the Captain's table!) together with two other people they'd met during the cruise. She was anxious to get a table for six in the dining room and during the speeches she kept moving, fairly discreetly, towards the door. Edward and Derek pretended not to notice so Mary-Jane and I ended up at the dining room "saving" them a space. The other couple were pleasant and it transpired that he knew Peter Smith and had completed a Ph.D. with him. Derek was impressed as he achieved this from a non-academic background, which is not easy.

It was a very good meal and occasion and later we met up with the diners from top table to hear how they got on, which was very well.

By 7.30 the following day we had arrived in Istanbul and had berthed in the commercial berth a little way from the centre of town. At 8.30 we set of on a trip of Old Istanbul which, although we had done it before, we were looking forward to doing it again. We were dropped off in St. Sophia Square which we remembered but, as with other places we have returned to, we were amazed at the crowds, not only of tourists (there were 100s) but also of hawkers of books, kilims, jewellery, water and bagels carried on a long stick.

We went across the gardens to the Blue Mosque, which still had the power to move and amaze as we looked at its silhouette of leaded domes cascading down from the one main dome and the six tall slender minarets, each with two or three balconies clinging on, standing tall and guarding the mosque itself. It was built in the early 1600s, taking only seven years to complete. It remains an important centre of Muslim worship and until recently 16 muezzins made the call to prayer, one from each balcony.

We entered through the enclosed courtyard surrounded by columned arcades, where washing now takes place. In the centre is a fountain, once the site where the ritual ablutions took place. In one of the arcades we duly had to remove our shoes and put them in the plastic bag provided. That was a change from the usual procedure outside a mosque of removing ones shoes and abandoning them, hoping they'll still be there when one emerges.

Inside is awash with light, from the many arched windows on several levels right up to the dome and from the huge chandeliers. The main central dome and all the semi domes around *and* all the columns are beautifully decorated with (Iznik) tiles, mainly blue of course, and with carving and fluting on the columns. In keeping with Islamic tradition the decoration has no depiction of human or animal but the flowers and plants are gorgeous. The whole interior is carpeted in blue and marked out to designate the places for prayer for the faithful, who are, on their knees.

To get to the Aya Sophia we walked through the Hippodrome, once the scene of chariot races now the scene of tourists and sellers. There are two obelisks in the square; only the top third of one remains after it was dropped in the docks and broken into four pieces in the 3rd-entury AD. It sits, now, on four blocks of stone. The hieroglyphs carved on it look as though they were carved this year not in the 16th century. The second obelisk, the Brazen Obelisk, was also erected in 390 AD and was clad in bronze, which was stolen and melted down for bullion in the fourth crusade.

There was a huge queue to get into Aya Sophia but as we were a group we were able to avoid this and got in fairly quickly. It claims to be one of the great buildings of the world; built as a long chamber and in the centre rather fine bronze doors, the entrance to the church and guarding the Imperial gate used only by the Emperor.

The interior is massive and awe inspiring. First of all you see the huge dome supported by four piers, the lower sections of which are bonded by lead not mortar, which support great arches which in turn are supporting the dome in which there are 40 windows. The ceiling is still mostly covered in gold mosaic probably from the 6th century and every bit as spectacular as it was then. It is embellished with designs of simple crosses edged with leaves and a geometric border.

A series of columns hold up the gallery; they have delicately carved capitals of vine leaves. Hanging from the gallery are large blue and gilt Islamic roundels which covered the faces of the mosaic saints. Also in the time it was a mosque marble platforms were put in for the muezzin, a mihrab and minbar and the floor of the apse was slightly reoriented so it faced Mecca.

The mosaics that remain are among the most important. One at the lower level is in the eastern apse and is of the Virgin and Child; in this mosaic she has a young and frail face, a very human depiction of her. To see the other renowned mosaics (and the ones Christine told us not to miss) are on the upper gallery which meant we had to negotiate the long ramp from the vestibule. The gallery was originally reserved for the women; the empress's throne was placed between two green columns which still stand and show traces of green.

The south wing is divided by a fine marble screen carved with keys and locks to look like a wooden door! Beyond this we saw the beautiful 13th-century mosaic of Christ in Majesty with the Virgin and St. John who was shown with a massive beard and wild hair! We walked to the far end of the gallery where several other mosaics have survived. One of them showed Christ with an Emperor and his wife who was covered in jewels and her third husband. The name and face had previously been erased, suggesting originally the figure was of a previous husband!

It was on then to the museum of Turkish and Islamic art; we went with some reluctance but the collection was quite small and accessible. The exhibits included fantastic calligraphy in striking designs; amazing golden Korans; decorative lanterns and pottery with colourful designs of leaves and flowers. We were delighted to have seen the museum and very glad we hadn't opted out.

We walked back to St. Sophia's square to wait for one of the buses taking us back to Minerva.

It had been a really good morning but the afternoon was, unexpectedly, even better. We were booked on a tour called

"Byzantine". It was to discover the Byzantine heritage of Istanbul. First it was the little Aghia Sophia Mosque built in 530s as an eastern orthodox church later converted into a mosque. It is one of the oldest Byzantine buildings in Istanbul; built of bricks set in thick mortar and with chains of small stone blocks with a big umbrella dome. The outside was of most importance from the point of view of Byzantine architecture. Inside it was light with its blue and white decoration and sunlight pouring in through the windows. It was typical of any mosque; a lower carpeted floor and a balconied gallery above and beautifully executed script from the Koran.

The next visit was to the spectacular cisterns, a huge underground reservoir built in 532 AD to provide water for the residents of Istanbul even if the city was besieged. There was some water in the reservoir, a tiny amount compared what could actually be held there but allowing the lights to be reflected creating a super atmosphere. In the water were a number of large, well fed carp. We walked along the board walks to look at the variety of columns that had been used by the builders and the column capitals of the head of Medusa set on its side or upside down! Those constructing the cisterns used up any derelict material; a very old example of recycling!

Finally it was to the museum of Chora, the museum of mosaic and frescoes. Again it too was built as a church and converted to a mosque; there was no alteration to the architecture except to add a minaret. It was changed to a museum in the 1950s and the whitewash and plaster were removed with great care from the mosaics and frescoes so we can appreciate the glories that had been hidden.

It is impossible to describe the mosaics and their visual impact. The entire interior of the chapel is covered in the glorious and detailed mosaics. Entering the church into the narthex we could follow the journey of the Holy family to Bethlehem, the census and onto the birth of Christ. Further on there were some of the miracles of Christ and then strangely the Magi going to Jerusalem and their audience with Herod. Up the south side were lots of the healing miracles

Inside the church the two domes depict the ancestors of Christ and of the Virgin; huge and with intriguing detail of their forebears. The faces in the mosaics were really life like and full of character. It was an absolutely brilliant visit and a very good one to finish on.

We had booked tickets for the shuttle bus back into the centre of town but with packing to do we decided against going and instead had a leisurely dinner, a chat with Mary-Jane, Edward, Sheila and Derek and finally a walk round the promenade deck, final packing and so to bed

This was going to be a long day; we were up at 5am by British time and we had to be out of our cabin by 8.40 a.m. local time and were faced with a dilemma – breakfastm then clear the cabin or clear, then breakfast? We chose the first option, went up to Veranda café and found a queue we had to join! It wasn't too long and we were soon seated with the Bishop and his wife (a rather formidable lady). They were good company and Derek and the bishop found they had a mutual acquaintance from school, Michael Henshaw, (a vicar in Warrington?). As a result of chatting we were late leaving breakfast and our cabin.

We then had a long and dreary wait in overcrowded conditions; it was cold and grey outside so there wasn't an opportunity to sit on deck for anyone, hence the crowding. There was the odd break for coffee, chats and lunch. One of the chats was to Sheila about our parties to be held in June and another to a lady who was staying on for the next cruise and was very excited about sailing into Venice.

After a good, and unexpected, lunch disembarkation began. We were the last of eight coaches to leave for the airport. Here there were the usual formalities and queues and waiting around but eventually we heard the flight announcement and set off. We found we were among the first to arrive at the gate but were bemused when we were directed to a deserted area. were we in the right place? Others were going straight on. Oh dear. Anyway eventually familiar faces arrived and we felt more reassured. It seemed that it was a ploy to distribute people around. The request to board was made, at least we thought it was, we couldn't hear, but there was, as usual, a mass movement and confusion.

Once all were on board we were off bound for London. It was a good flight above the clouds; a good meal and landing. The collection of cases and transfer to the Manchester flight, though our hearts sank at the length of the passport queues but they moved quickly and we were entertained by the number of people who triggered the alarm on the security arch, that was until Derek did so he had to be frisked and remove his shoes. On the final leg of the flight we were again with the elderly, single lady who had been on the flight down. It turned out she was from Windermere and a taxi would be waiting at

Manchester to run her home.

We claimed our bags and had the usual exchange from the taxi driver about the charge to Styal. We assured him we realised what we had to pay but he insisted he couldn't charge us that amount and reduced it a lot; this earned him a generous tip, which he was surprisingly reluctant to take!

Feelings about the cruise

Some disappointments: The weather; missing Monemvasia (a big disappointment); missing Delos (again) and Tinos; not getting up to see the early birds; not many birds!

The good things: The excursions were very good especially the Acropolis museum; Kayakoy village; the flowers and the botany trips; Ephesus and the Chora church/museum; lectures; some very pleasant dinner companions.

In spite of sentiments expressed We think we will sail with Minerva again. There isn't any ship we like better and on the whole it suits us both. So here's to the next one!

Chapter 12

Iceland. All in one day

A few years ago the Iceland Tourism Authority organised a scheme whereby one could fly from Manchester to Iceland, have a tour and fly back in the evening, We were intrigued,so the day came when the alarm went at 4.a.m and we drove to Manchester Airport to board the plane and have a pretty good breakfast before we were losing height to land in Iceland, "The land of ice and fire", at 7.30 a.m. local time. We were allocated to Tour 1 and were whisked off to The Blue Lagoon, so called because of effluent from a local power station. Rocks around the lagoon were slimy with white silica deposits. The whole area is volcanic and with lava that was moss covered and looked like a moonscape; when American astronauts were preparing to walk on the moon, they came here to simulate the conditions.

After coffee, and swimming for a few, we set off over the mountains, which are only open in the summer; from September to May, frequently icy and closed by snow. We made a brief stop at a water-filled crater that was caused by an eruption of a volcanic fissure, which was 55 metres deep, before pausing for a "comfort stop" at "Eden", which was full of plants grown in a geothermal climate courtesy of the thermal power stations The Great Guyser has been active since June 2,000 but only occasionally and fortunately not during our visit. The Stoker Guyser was blowing every five minutes. It was a strange area; really atmospheric, but very wet!

We had lunch in a not very salubrious snack bar and then it was back onto the coach to drive to Gullfloss, a magnificent white river and a huge, wide waterfall that drops 32 metres. Apparently in 1907 an Englishman tried to buy the falls, but the daughter of a local Bratholt farmer fought against it. But she lost her case, however the lease was not paid, so the ownership of the falls reverted to Iceland, where it remains.

The next stop was Pingvellir, a national park of historical significance as it includes the "Law Mountain", where laws were made and then pronounced in front of assembled civic representatives on the assembly field at the base of the mountain, where there is a flat area due to a rift between the European and north American tectonic plates. it has been a place of assembly since 930 AD called "The Althing". Here legal disputes were settled, marriages were made or arranged and laws made. The river was re-routed to enclose the assembly field and a large beautiful lake was created. We had a very welcome walk around in the dry and with some sunshine.

Next was the last leg of our tour to the capital Reykjavik, passing the harbour with it's marine research vessels and whalers, then to Tjorn, a large pond in the centre of town with lots of birds and water fowl and a visit to "The Pearl", basically water storage tanks from the power stations, but developed into an amenity with restaurants and wonderful views, so we could see the huge

Lutheran church Hallgrimskyurkja, which took 34 years to build from 1940 to 1974.

Then it was back to the airport, passing the impressive university before boarding the plane for the return flight to Manchester, enjoying dinner on the way. We drove home feeling somewhat tired after a fascinating day in this land of 200 volcanoes and a cold climate ranging from -3 Celcius in January to 11 Celcius in July. It has a long history of civilisation and lawmaking with the world's first parliament, the Althing. Their total population is 370,000, of whom a third are under 39. Although they are a member of Nato, they have no military forces of their own, but there is an American army base adjoining the airport where we landed.. We are not likely to return, but are very glad we went.

Printed in Great Britain
by Amazon